Celebrate!

DAILY DEVOTIONS *for the* SPIRIT-FILLED LIFE

Jack W. Hayford
Sam Middlebrook

THOMAS NELSON PUBLISHERS
Nashville

CELEBRATE! Daily Devotions for the Spirit-Filled Life

Acknowledgments

The Publishers and Dr. Jack W. Hayford wish to acknowledge with gratitude the "team" who joined to make this inspiring devotional possible. Midway in its production, Dr. Sam Middlebrook, co-author of this book and life-long friend and ministerial associate of Pastor Hayford, was promoted to his heavenly reward. In the wake of his sudden homegoing, this project was brought to completion through the skilled and dedicated effort of Rebecca Bauer's editorial enterprise. Further, we thank Dr. John Amstutz and Dr. Nathaniel Van Cleave, along with Scott Bauer, Doug and Denise Hammack and Bill Middlebrook for their written contributions to this "medley of meditations."

Table of Contents

Celebrate!

DAILY DEVOTIONS
for the
SPIRIT-FILLED LIFE

January

The Word of God

New Beginnings

Man lives by every word that proceeds from the mouth of the Lord.
Deuteronomy 8:3

At the beginning of His earthly ministry Jesus quoted this text in Matthew 4:4, when He faced Satan's snares in the wilderness. By doing so He made the knowledge of the Word a powerful weapon against the attack of the adversary. Because the parallel is used of Israel's receiving the daily supply of manna, we know that the believer is to seek and feed upon a regular, daily portion of God's Word. Psalm 119:165 adds that the Word of God has provided for us a solid base that will keep us firm and secure no matter what circumstance we face.

Let no one suppose spiritual survival is possible for long without nourishment from the Word of God. First Peter 2:2 declares that God's Word is as essential to the believer as milk to a newborn child. It is not an option!

As you begin your ministry this year, are you drawing daily on the Word? It is a discoverable, definitive, discerning resource for meeting every challenge. Whatever you face this year, God's promises are there, for you.

Laws for Living

Forever, O Lord, Your word is settled in heaven. You established the earth, and it abides. Psalm 119:90, 91

Though times and seasons change, though social customs, human opinions, and philosophical viewpoints vary, they have no effect on the constancy or authority of God's Word.

Just as He spoke and the earth was created and is sustained, so He has spoken regarding His laws for living. The relativism of human thought does not affect His authority or standards. However, whatever our past rebellion, when we come to Christ, we need to make God's Word the governing principle for our life. Jesus conclusively declares this in John 8:47, "He who is of God hears God's words." James 1:22 further exhorts us to "be doers of the word, and not hearers only." The word we hear will ultimately require action.

Where does the Word need to be applied in our lives today? As we hear and yield to the authority of God's Word, we verify that we are no longer dominated by the world's spirit of error (1 John 4:6), but are applying the power, promise, and blessing of His Word to our lives.

The Word of God

New Creation

[We have] been born again, not of corruptible seed but incorruptible, through the word of God which lives and abides forever.

1 Peter 1:23

Just as we owe our natural existence to the Creator's spoken word and life-giving breath, so we owe our spiritual existence to the power of God's Word and the Holy Spirit's activation of its power.

God's intent for our created being is completely fulfilled only when our spirits are alive toward Him. This text tells us that the "seed" that has produced new life in us is the *Word* of God, which has begotten us by the Holy Spirit's power and made us members of God's new creation.

That new creation is an ongoing phenomenon in each of our lives. And the power of God's Word is in no way more manifest than in this: its power to bring spiritual life to all who are open to its truth in *every* area of life.

Is there an area in our lives that seems lifeless or stagnant? Let us allow the Holy Spirit to plant the "seed" of the Word in that realm of our life and then watch as His life flows anew through us.

The Word of God

Obedience

He who has My commandments and keeps them, it is he who loves Me.

John 14:21

Jesus completely aligned His life and will with the Father's, indicating His total allegiance to the Father's Word and commandments. He also disapproved of any attitude that would teach less than full obedience to the entirety of God's revealed Word.

Thus, in this text, Jesus explicitly links His disciples' love for Him as Savior with their will to keep His commandments: If we love Him, we will love His Father's Word, also.

In John 5:39, our Lord declares that the knowledge of the Scriptures is the pathway to knowing Him well. Further, upon His resurrection, He unveiled the fullness of His own Person as revealed in the Old Testament (Luke 24:27). These texts cluster to teach us to *follow* Christ, to *know* Him, and to *grow* in insight as people walking with the resurrected Lord.

A basic and continuing requirement to seeing this accomplished is a steadfast commitment to hearing, heeding, and studying the Bible. Step into its wonders today!

The Word of God

Fruitfulness

*[My word] shall not return to Me void, but it shall accomplish
what I please, and it shall prosper.*   Isaiah 55:11

Evangelism (the spreading of the Good News) and
expansion (the enlarging of life's potential under
God) both multiply by the "seed" of God's Word. Jesus also
described the Word as "seed"—the source of all saving life
and growth possibilities coming from the Father to
mankind.

Whether we come to Him with a spiritual need, physical
need, or emotional need, all increase of life within His love
comes by His Word, as human response gives room for His
blessing to happen. When received, God's word of promise
will never be barren. The power in His Word will always
fulfill the promise of His Word. We never need wonder
how faith is developed or how fruitfulness is realized.

Fruitfulness is the guaranteed by-product of God's Word—
whether for the salvation of a lost soul or the provision of a
disciple's need. God's Word cannot be barren or fruitless—
His own life-power is within it!

Guidance

Your word is a lamp to my feet and a light to my Path.

Psalm 119:105

*A*ll of us are too inexperienced to try to make it through life without a guide. God's Word is that guide. Psalm 119 unfolds the manifold features of God's Word, showing how dynamically and practically it will assist us in all of life's circumstances. But no single verse focuses this more clearly than verse 105, which shows how God's Word lights the way, giving direction for each *step* ("to my feet") and giving wisdom for *long-range* plans ("to my path").

Joshua links the regular application of God's Word to life as the most certain way to both success and prosperity in living (Josh. 1:8). Further, Psalm 119:130 notes the wisdom God's Word gives to the "simple," reminding us not to make decisions based on human delusion or outright senselessness. Also, Proverbs 6:23 reminds us that the reproofs of God are essential and for life.

Let God's Word guide, correct, instruct, lead, teach, and confirm. Do not hasten ahead without it —*ever.*

The Word of God

Purity

He who looks into the perfect law of liberty and continues in it
. . . will be blessed in what he does.   *James 1:25*

Purity of life is not a quest for perfection as much as it is a quest for liberation from those things that may inhibit effectiveness and reduce power-filled living. This text shows the Word of God as a means of reflection—a mirror into which we are to look and see ourselves. The call is not only to heed what we see and accept the Bible's corrective instruction, but there is an unwritten lesson here. We should avoid the temptation to see (and judge) others in the Word, analyzing what they ought to do, instead of what *we* need to do.

Second Corinthians 3:18 also likens God's Word to a mirror, but describes the picture seen as no less than the Lord Jesus Himself. Thus, the Bible shows us Christ's likeness in order that we may measure our conduct and character against His and allow God to shape us into Christ's image.

Today, ask the Lord to use His Word in your life so that you will "be conformed to the image of His Son" (Rom. 8:29).

Unashamed Workers

Be diligent to present yourself approved to God, a worker who does not need to be ashamed, rightly dividing the word of truth.
2 Timothy 2:15

The Bible, God's inspired Word, is the only conclusive source of wisdom, knowledge, and understanding of ultimate realities. It is a fountainhead of truth and a gold mine of practical principles, waiting to liberate and enrich the person who will pursue its truth and wealth.

Thus, Paul's instruction to "be diligent . . . a worker" has been applied by serious Christians through the centuries as a directive to study the Word of God. The only way to healthy, balanced living is through "rightly dividing" God's Word. Such application of God's Word is the result of diligent study.

Psalm 119:11 further urges memorizing the Word of God as a mighty deterrent against sin. Memorizing the Scripture also provides an immediate availability of God's words as a sword, ready in witnessing and effective in spiritual warfare.

As we continue to pour God's Word into our hearts, let it "dwell in [us] richly" (Col. 3:16) today.

The Word of God

The God-Breathed Word

All Scripture is given by inspiration of God . . . that the man of God may be complete, thoroughly equipped for every good work.
2 Timothy 3:16, 17

The absolute authority of the Bible over our lives is based on the fact that this Book does not merely *contain* the Word of God, but that it *is* the Word of God in its sum and in its parts.

The Greek translated "inspiration of God," literally means "God-breathed," describing the Bible's origin as transcending human inspiration. The Bible is not the product of elevated human consciousness or enlightened human intellect. It is not merely the private opinion of the writer (2 Pet. 1:20), but is directly "breathed" from God Himself.

This text further teaches us the purpose of Scripture: "that the man of God may be complete, thoroughly equipped for every good work." The same Lord who sent His Word to us so faithfully is beside us today, to equip us. Let us fearlessly step out into His glorious plan for our lives. We are not going in our own resource. He is completing us, maturing us, and equipping us through His Word.

The Eternal Word

Till heaven and earth pass away, one jot or one tittle will by no means pass from the law till all is fulfilled.   Matthew 5:18

As the resurrected King, God's Messiah and our Savior, our Lord Jesus Christ has given us some of the most important statements concerning the authority and dependability of the Word of God.

Jesus confirms the truth that *every word* of the Scriptures is given by God. He goes so far as to make direct reference to the smallest letter, "jot," and the smallest punctuation point, "tittle."

Further, when He says "the Scripture cannot be broken" (John 10:35), He is describing the utter inviolability of God's Word from man's side (do not try to diminish its truth or meaning) and the utter dependability of it from God's side (He will uphold it—His Word will not dissolve or be shaken). All creation may dissolve, but God's Word will stand forever (Matt. 24:35)!

The Word of God

On Christian Maturity

I fed you with milk and not with solid food; for until now you were not able to receive it.   *1 Corinthians 3:2*

*B*eginning in 1 Corinthians 2:10, Paul elaborates our need of wisdom and revelation from the Holy Spirit, and he ties this very firmly to our receiving the "words . . . which the Holy Spirit teaches" (2:13). He immediately turns from these observations to an outright confrontation with the carnality of the Corinthians, attributing it to the shallowness of their understanding of God's Word. Hebrews 5:12–14 elaborates this by asserting that "everyone who partakes only of milk is unskilled in the word of righteousness."

The demanding truth of this passage is that no amount of supposed insight or experience reflects genuine spiritual growth if it is not rooted in the knowledge of God's Word. Such "rootedness" is in *truth* and *love,* not merely in learned knowledge or accomplished study. In order to experience true spiritual growth, we must spend time in the Word.

Just as a baby requires food to grow, so we require the daily input of God's Word for our spiritual growth (1 Pet. 2:2). Let us make study of the Word a priority in our lives and see how it begins to "grow" in us!

The Word of God

January 12

His Complete Word

The law of the Lord is perfect.   Psalm 19:7

That the "law of the Lord is perfect" refers to the absolute, complete, and entire trustworthiness of the Holy Scriptures. The Word of God is *perfect* in its accuracy and *sure* in its dependability. The Bible is unfailing as an absolutely trustworthy guide for our faith (belief in God) and practice (life and behavior).

This text goes on to describe the completeness of Scripture to meet our every need. It brings us salvation, wisdom, joy, insight, truth, and righteousness.

Whatever we may be facing today, let us look to God's Word for guidance. It is a sure source we can rely on in times of need. This is so because God is *true,* because His Word reveals His truth, and because God cannot lie. Deuteronomy 7:9 confirms this: "Therefore know that the Lord your God, He is God, the faithful God who keeps covenant . . . with those who love Him and keep His commandments."

The Word of God

His Sufficient Word

You shall not add to the word which I command you, nor take away from it.   *Deuteronomy 4:2*

The Bible is completely trustworthy and sufficient to answer anything we need to know for eternal salvation. It is also a sure source of practical wisdom concerning our relationships, morality, character, or conduct.

The Bible warns against either adding to or subtracting from its contents. Revelation 22:18 is a clear warning against adding to God's Word. A classic study of the judgment for taking away from God's Word is seen in Jeremiah 36:20–32. Wise is the one who says, "Add to or subtract from the Bible at your own risk."

Though many books are inspiring, they can only reflect the consummate order of divine revelation as found in the Scriptures. The fog of confusion that can arise from a casual or gullible attitude toward these books dissipates in the burning light of the Word of God.

Let's make the Bible our court of first resort!

Ministering in Love

The letter kills, but the Spirit gives life.   *2 Corinthians 3:6*

*B*elieving in the truthfulness of God's Word does not guarantee that we will minister that truth in the Spirit of God. Ephesians 4:15 describes growth and maturity in the body of Christ as characterized by our "speaking the truth in love," and Proverbs 18:21 warns us that life and death are in the tongue.

Our Lord challenges us to maintain the constant presence of His life in the things we speak, even in the most demanding declarations of correction or judgment. Urgency may attend our message and passion infuse our delivery; but anger, impatience, and irritation are not of the life-giving Spirit, however literally accurate our interpretation of the Bible may be.

The psalmist prayed, "Let the words of my mouth . . . be acceptable in Your sight," and Proverbs 16:1 tells us that the "answer of the tongue is from the Lord." When we face a situation where words "just don't seem to be enough," we need to turn to the Lord and let Him speak His Word through us.

The Word of God

Truth that Frees

You shall know the truth, and the truth shall make you free.
John 8:32

We often expect freedom to come to us with little effort on our part. We function as though our initial birth into God's family is the only step we need take to see all of His inheritance realized in our lives. But this text clearly states that it is through knowing the truth that freedom is born. That places the requirement on us to constantly seek to know more of God's truth as found in His Word.

The Greek word used here for "know" literally means to perceive, understand, recognize, gain knowledge, realize, or come to know. It implies a knowledge that has an inception, a progress, and an attainment. We can know the truth of God intellectually without ever applying it to our lives, but the knowledge spoken of here is the recognition of truth by personal experience.

What areas of our lives need to be freed? The Word of God has an answer for us. As we tap into this resource, and apply it to our lives, the Lord will bring us into freedom.

The Word of God

Peace

Great peace have those who love Your law, and nothing causes them to stumble.   Psalm 119:165

*P*eace—it is the ever-elusive, all-consuming desire of every person. It always seems just beyond our reach and an impossible goal in a world gone mad. But this Scripture gives a promise for peace that can easily be realized by anyone. It says that if we love God's Word, we *will* have peace.

The word for "peace" used here is the well-known Hebrew word *shalom*. We tend to think of *shalom* merely as a simple greeting. It does, of course, mean peace, safety, and tranquility. Yet inherent in the meaning of the word is completeness, wholeness, health, prosperity, fullness, rest, and harmony. Thus peace is much more than the absence of war and conflict; it is the wholeness that the entire human race seeks.

Where do we need the wholeness of God's peace in our lives? As we fall in love with His Word, peace will naturally be the by-product.

The Word of God

Laws for Living

You . . . gave them just ordinances and true laws, good statutes and commandments.   Nehemiah 9:13

The Hebrew noun used here for "statutes" means an enactment, an inscription; a written rule, decreed limit, law, or custom. It refers to a defined boundary, especially when written into law, but sometimes not in written form, as in God's limits for the sea (Prov. 8:29).

While we all know that statutes are given for our benefit, we sometimes find ourselves going beyond their limits when there is no one nearby to enforce them. Unfortunately, we do the same thing with God's law—usually to our own detriment. Yet, unlike manmade laws, God's laws are never arbitrary or inconsistent. God's laws come directly from the Creator's hand and are, in essence, a "how-to" book for the human race!

Do we need guidance today? Listen for His voice. Are we facing one of life's uncertainties? The answer is in the Word. Is there something in our lives that needs to be fixed? When we don't know what to do, we look it up in the manual!

January 18

Bread of Life

And they told . . . how [Jesus] was known to them in the breaking of bread.
                                                    Luke 24:35

One of the most tender accounts in the Bible is that of Jesus meeting the disciples on the road to Emmaus. His patience and love in explaining the Scriptures to them is worth noting for our own benefit.

Break thou the bread of life, dear Lord, to me,
As thou didst break the loaves beside the sea;
Beyond the sacred page I seek thee, Lord;
My spirit pants for thee, O living Word.

Thou art the bread of life, O Lord, to me,
Thy holy Word the truth that saveth me;
Give me to eat and live with thee above;
Teach me to love thy truth, for thou art love.

O send thy Spirit, Lord, now unto me,
That he may touch mine eyes, and make me see:
Show me the truth concealed within thy Word,
And in thy Book revealed I see thee, Lord.

Let us read our Bible with Jesus today; He's waiting to open the Scriptures to us!

The Word of God

Believe the Word

I believe Your commandments.   Psalm 119:66
And they believed the Scripture.   John 2:22

The Greek and Hebrew words for "believe" combine to give us a picture of faith that not only requires our participation, but provides us a foundation upon which we can stand and be established.

Pisteuo is the Greek verb form of the word here used for believe. It means to trust in, have faith in, be fully convinced of, and rely on. It expresses reliance upon something and a personal trust that produces obedience. The Hebrew word here used for believe is *'aman* and means to be firm, stable, established, and firmly persuaded. In 2 Chronicles 20:20 the word appears three times and could be translated: "Be established in the Lord . . . and you will be established."

The key to being established in the Lord is becoming grounded in His Word. Does our faith seem weak? Faith comes by hearing the Word of God (Rom. 10:17). Do we sometimes feel as if our life is built on shifting sand? Let us build our lives on Jesus—the Word (John 1:14). And, as we believe in the Lord, we will be established.

For Children's Sake

And these words which I command you today shall be in your heart. You shall teach them diligently to your children.

Deuteronomy 6:6, 7

The Word of God is the basis for all successful family relationships, whether with parents, siblings, or spouse. This text, however, deals with the foundation we must lay in raising our children to be people of God. We are to begin by instructing them in the Word.

Following God's law is not given to make us into spiritual crackpots, but rather to make us "naturally supernatural." Living God's Word doesn't require that we tack Scripture placards all over our walls and speak in a "holy" tone of voice. It does require, however, that we teach our children how to apply God's Word to appropriate situations (Prov. 4:1–4; 1 Cor. 10:11). It does require that we fill our homes with the joy of the Lord (Neh. 8:10). It does require that we follow the structure that God has ordained within a believing home (Eph. 5:22—6:4). And it does require consistency and persistence in teaching (2 Tim. 3:14–17).

What are we to do when we face a challenge in our family? We apply the Word, and watch the Lord turn the situation to His glory.

The Word of God

Memorize the Word

Bind them continually upon your heart . . . For the command-
ment is a lamp, and the law a light.   *Proverbs 6:21, 23*

This text charges us to *continually* bind the commandments of the Lord upon our hearts. The Hebrew
word for "continually" means constantly, evermore, or per-
petually. The primary idea is of something permanent and
unceasing.

This leaves no doubt that making God's Word a part of our
lives is to be a primary occupation of the believer. We are
to *continually* hide God's Word in our hearts. Scripture
exhorts us to hide His words in our hearts (Ps. 119:11), and
to "let the word of Christ dwell in you richly" so that we can
teach and admonish one another (Col. 3:16). As we do this,
God's Word not only opens avenues of ministry, but it also
becomes our guide (Ps. 73:23, 24), our defense (Eph. 6:17),
our refuge (Ps. 91:2), our standard of faith (1 Thess. 2:13),
and our comfort (John 15:26).

Whatever the Lord ministers to us today from His Word,
let us bind it to our heart. Memorize it. Meditate on it.
Minister it.

The Word—Part 1

Let the word of Christ dwell in you richly.   Colossians 3:16

The definitions of the two principal words translated "word" in Scripture give us an understanding of the Word of God in our lives.

Logos is a transmission of thought, a word of explanation, an oracle, or divine revelation. *Davar* means a word, a speech, a matter, or thing. Note the similarity between the Hebrew *davar* and the Greek *logos*. Jesus is the living *Logos* (John 1:1), the Bible is the written *logos* (Heb. 4:12), and the Holy Spirit utters the spoken *logos* (1 Cor. 2:13). Jesus is the *Davar* of the Old Testament, and the *Logos* of the New Testament. He is the message of the entire book.

Jesus became the physical embodiment of the Word of God—in much the same way God wants to dwell within each of us. As we study the Scriptures today, let us ask the Lord how He wants to fill us with His Word.

The Word—Part 2

Man shall not live by bread alone, but by every word that pro-
ceeds from the mouth of God.   Matthew 4:4

*I*n contrast to *logos,* the Greek word *rhema* means that
which is said or spoken, an utterance. Though both
are translated "word," they have radically different mean-
ings. *Logos* is the message; *rhema* is the communication of
the message. In reference to the Bible, *logos* is the Bible in
its entirety; *rhema* is an individual verse. The meaning of
rhema in distinction to *logos* is illustrated in Ephesians 6:17,
where the reference is not to the Scriptures as a whole, but
to that portion which the believer wields as a sword in the
time of need.

The Hebrew word most similar in meaning to *rhema* is
'imrah, which means speech, word, commandment, or
answer. In Psalm 119, *'imrah* occurs twenty-one times,
including verse 11: "Your word I have hidden in my heart,
that I might not sin against You."

Both words emphasize the importance of the individual
Scriptures used in time of need. Is there an area in our
lives where trial threatens or sin tempts? Take the
Scripture as a sword and stand strong in His might.

The Perfect Law

But he who looks into the perfect law of liberty and continues in it, . . . this one will be blessed in what he does.   *James 1:25*

"The law of the Lord is perfect," the psalmist asserted. And in this text, James reaffirms that the law of liberty in which we live is truly *perfect*.

The Greek word for "perfect" used here in James is *teleios*. *Teleios* refers to that which fulfills its purpose. In other words, it is something that is finished, completed—perfect. When applied to persons, it signifies consummate soundness and includes the idea of being whole. More particularly, when applied to believers, it denotes maturity.

James further adds that we are not only to "continue in" the Word, but we are also to give ourselves in ministry. It is this two-pronged focus—the Word and the work—that brings about that *perfect* maturity and soundness in our lives.

We give ourselves to the reading and study of the Word. Then we ask the Lord to open doors of ministry to us. He wants to bring His perfection to our lives today.

The Word of God

Nourishment

As newborn babes, desire the pure milk of the word, that you may grow thereby.

1 Peter 2:2

The Word of God has been given to us as the most basic requirement of our spiritual growth. Regular reading and consistent study are to us as milk is to an infant, providing us with nourishment for growth, liquid to quench our thirst, and antibodies to help us fight the disease of sin.

Other Scriptures emphasize the importance of the Word as our principal source of spiritual nourishment.

Job 23:12 encourages us to prioritize the Word over all other distractions—even our most basic physical needs. We are admonished to consume more of the Word as we grow, just like a child whose need for food increases as he grows (Heb. 5:12–14). And like an elated child who sees dinner being put on the table, Jeremiah exults that the Word was his source of joy (Jer. 15:16).

As we open our Bibles today, we don't need to be bashful! Let us eat until we are full! He has the banquet all prepared.

Cleansing

. . . that He might sanctify and cleanse her with the washing of water by the word. *Ephesians 5:25, 26*

This text makes clear that Jesus has an ongoing commitment to our growth in holiness. In John 17:17, He prays *for* us with the words, "Sanctify them by Your truth. Your word is truth." Our Lord is not only committed to us, but is interceding on our behalf. Yet while our purification from sin and strength for ongoing holiness can come only from His hand, a large part of the responsibility for seeing our lives made pure rests squarely on our shoulders.

The psalmist asks the question, "How can a young man cleanse his way?" Then immediately answers, "By taking heed according to Your word" (119:9). The Word, therefore, becomes the key to seeing that constant cleansing take place.

Where does cleansing need to take place in our lives today? As we rest in Jesus and on the Word, let us echo the commitment of 2 Corinthians 7:1, "Therefore, having these promises, beloved, let us cleanse ourselves from all filthiness of the flesh and spirit, perfecting holiness in the fear of God."

The Word of God

Sword of the Word

And take the helmet of salvation, and the sword of the Spirit, which is the word of God.   *Ephesians 6:17*

What a comfort, in the midst of the trials and temptations of daily living, to know that the Lord has not left us without defense. In every circumstance the adversary has planned against us, we have been given the power of the Word of God to fight off the enemy, defend ourselves, and rescue others from the evil one. Hebrews 4:12 says that "the word of God is living and powerful and sharper than any two-edged sword."

Revelation 1:16 gives us further insight into the use of this weapon: "out of His [Jesus] mouth went a sharp two-edged sword." And Isaiah, speaking prophetically of the Messiah, says, "And He has made My mouth like a sharp sword." So as we wield the sword of the Word in battle, we are, in essence, speaking Jesus' words into the situation.

As we step into the fray, remember with confidence that our Commander not only gives us a place of safety and the confidence for battle, He then places the sword of His own Word in our hands.

Ready to Minister

So then faith comes by hearing, and hearing by the word of God.
Romans 10:17

The relationship between the input of the Word and the growth of our faith is striking. This text goes so far as to suggest that they cannot be separated! That places us under great accountability, not only in the area of our own Bible study, but in how we speak the Word to those around us.

Second Samuel 23:2 says, "The Spirit of the Lord spoke by me, and His word was on my tongue." And 1 Peter 3:15 exhorts us to "always be ready to give a defense to everyone who asks you a reason for the hope that is in you." We are to be ready at all times to speak a word of life into any circumstance and to give an explanation of our faith to anyone who asks.

We are not always able to plan ahead for those occasions. So we let our times in the Word build our faith that we may truly "be ready in season and out of season" (2 Tim. 4:2) to exhort and teach.

The Word of God

His Promises

There has not failed one word of all His good promise.
1 Kings 8:56

God has given us many promises. He gives the promise to restore the things in our past (Joel 2:25, 26). He gives us promises concerning today (Ps. 23:6). And He gives promises for our future, both here on earth and eternally with Him (2 Pet. 3:13).

As we read through our Bible, let us take note of the profusion of blessings God promises His people! Second Corinthians 1:20 says that "all the promises of God in Him are Yes, and in Him Amen, to the glory of God through us." That means that no matter what our past has been, no matter what we are facing today, no matter how bleak our future may appear, every promise in Scripture is for *us*.

What promise do we need to claim today? No matter what area of life we are concerned about, rest assured His promise will not fail! We are "fully convinced that what He [has] promised He [is] able also to perform" (Rom. 4:21).

The Solid Rock

Whoever comes to Me, and hears My sayings . . . is like a man building a house on the rock.   Luke 6:47, 48

Just like the man in this Scripture, all of us want to build our lives on something that is solid, firm, and secure as stone. That "something" we seek is indeed a stone, and 1 Peter 2:6 declares that Christ is that cornerstone.

But this text also points out that the type of man we are to emulate is the one who hears the sayings of the Lord and does them. Those two facts cannot be separated: if we want to build our lives on Christ the chief cornerstone, we must hear and obey His Word.

When life seems to change as frequently as shifting sand, with altered circumstances, broken relationships, and fluctuating social standards, it is to the solid, rock-like foundation of Scripture we must turn.

With the psalmist, let us daily cry out: Lord, "lead me to the rock that is higher than I" (Ps. 61:2). That's the only sure place to build our lives!

The Word of God

Death to Life

. . . and the bones came together . . . and breath came into them, and they lived.

Ezekiel 37:7, 10

All of us face times when our lives seem as scorched and lifeless as Ezekiel's valley of dry bones. But as Ezekiel lifted his voice in speaking the Word of God, it became a mighty, life-giving force!

Centuries later, Jesus instructed His disciples: "The words that I speak to you are spirit, and they are life" (John 6:63). Later, following the birth of the church, these same disciples spent much of their time in the temple speaking "the words of this life" (Acts 5:20). They recognized the power of the life-giving Word of God!

Just ten chapters following the vision of the dry bones, Ezekiel is brought to the river of healing waters that bring God's life, health, and abundance wherever they go. God has the same blessing in store for each one of us, but it requires that we hold "fast the word of life, so that [we] may rejoice in the day of Christ" (Phil. 2:16).

The Word of God

February

The Way of Love

My Brother's Keeper

Then the Lord said to Cain, "Where is Abel your brother?" He said, "Am I my brother's keeper?"   *Genesis 4:9*

The Lord answers Cain's rhetorical question with a powerful call to account for his actions, his attitude, and his neglect of the mandate to "keep" his brother. If we were to ask the Lord the same question of our brothers and sisters, His answer would call us to account just as emphatically. We *do* have a mandate to care for, to nurture, and to "keep" those around us.

First, we *are* responsible for our natural families. How often we ignore the spiritual, emotional, and physical care of those to whom we are related.

Second, we *are* responsible for our spiritual families. We must regularly minister to our brothers, sisters, fathers, and mothers in the faith. Our attitudes toward them must reflect the care fitting the mandate our Lord gave us to "love one another."

Third, in the parable of the Good Samaritan, Jesus called us to nurture those we are not naturally disposed to like. What of those who rub us the wrong way? "Am I his keeper, Lord? Surely not, Father, you know how reprehensibly difficult he is; surely not him, Lord. . . ."

And our Lord answers.

The Way of Love

Forgiveness

And Joseph said to his brothers . . . , "I am Joseph your brother, whom you sold into Egypt."
                                           Genesis 45:4

Do you suppose that while Joseph was being sent to misery and an almost certain death in Egypt that he thought God was preparing him to rule a nation? I don't think so.

Do you suppose that while he was imprisoned in darkness and filth that he felt the anticipation of one preparing for a glorious future? I don't think so.

Do you suppose that during the long, forced march to Egypt he was thankful to his brothers for acting as the hand of God moving him toward the realization of his destiny? I don't think so.

Yet when Joseph forgave his brothers, he revealed a long-term attitude of heart that allowed his suffering to become his strength. God expects us to forgive because we're growing in Christ-like love. But more personally, when we forgive, we allow God to take the mean treatment we receive and turn it into the forging of a character that allows God to use us to rule in our own Egypt.

Who is God using to shape your character? Are you forgiving?

The Way of Love

Reaching to Others

The stranger who dwells among you shall be to you as one born among you, and you shall love him as yourself.　Leviticus 19:34

The young girl, with her family, moved from church to church with some regularity. It was always with pain that she moved into a new Sunday School. Feeling like an outsider was embarrassing. She didn't know the ropes, and it made her feel rejected before anybody even had the chance to reject her.

It's not just pre-adolescent self-consciousness that makes us feel that way. Every day in our churches, at our jobs, at the PTA, in our neighborhood, there are people feeling like outsiders.

Further, the brokenness of our society causes even those of us who seem "connected" to feel alienated from one another.

Our Lord *commands* us to be His representatives to integrate those who feel ostracized into the protecting greenhouse of His love and care. It's our arms that reach out for Him. It's our words that draw them in.

Are you reaching? To whom?

The Way of Love

Love Your Neighbor

Lord, who may abide in Your tabernacle? . . . He who does not backbite . . . nor does he take up a reproach against his friend.
                                                            Psalm 15:1, 3

The Lord's command that we love one another was not new with Jesus. For as long as the Lord has been revealing the pathway to walk with Him, love for our neighbor has been central.

While David was musing on God's qualifications for one to walk in communion with Him, the Lord spoke to him the same thing John would later reveal as central to the gospel: "for he who does not love his brother whom he has seen, how can he love God whom he has not seen?" (1 John 4:20).

Walking closely with God is synonymous with walking in harmony with those around us. Can we speak poorly of our brothers and sisters and walk closely with God? Can we criticize and condemn those we're commanded to love, and yet walk closely with God? It appears not.

Walking with God seems such a mystical concept; however, He's made it very easy for us to understand. If we want to walk close to Him, we must walk agreeably with one another.

The Way of Love

Forgiveness

For You, Lord, are good, and ready to forgive, and abundant in mercy to all those who call upon You.   Psalm 86:5

Scripture makes clear that, having received much from the hand of the Lord, much is expected of us (Luke 12:48). This is true of spiritual gifts, of cherished parental investment, of financial blessing, and of many other benefits we enjoy. What we do with what we've been given is very important to the Lord.

Nowhere is this truth more evident than the gift of merciful forgiveness the Lord extends to us all. Only you and the Lord can know how many the character flaws, how frequent the points of failure, how obvious the compromise, and how unholy the thoughts, all of which have been completely forgiven by the Holy Lord.

What will you do with so great a gift?

You have but one choice before the Lord—extend that same forgiveness in bucketsful to those who wrong you. When someone's character flaw brings you personal injury, you forgive. When their point of failure affects you personally, you forgive. When their unholy living brings you offense, you forgive.

Jesus extends mercy. Jesus forgives failure. Will we?

The Way of Love

Love the Unlovely

And when Jesus went out He saw a great multitude; and He was
moved with compassion for them.   Matthew 14:14

We have a world full of hurting people who need love. I am one. So are you. To some degree we have all been hurt. Maybe it is by selfish parents, or by uncaring institutions, or by cutting relationships, or by an isolating and alienating society, but we have all been hurt.

Jesus shows a love for hurting people: "and He was moved with compassion for them."

The Greek word used here for that loving compassion means literally "to have the bowels moved with great feeling." The deepest part of Jesus' emotional capacity was, and still is, turned in sincere feeling for the hurting of our world—you and me included.

Today, let us each ask the Lord to make us a reflection of Jesus' life, to make us sensitive to the hurts of those around us.

Are you willing to care like that? Is it your prayer to be made that way?

The Way of Love

Love the Unlovely

But if you love those who love you, what credit is that to you? For even sinners love those who love them.   Luke 6:32

What do you suppose your emotional response would be to someone who spoke a well-positioned lie that caused you to lose your career? What if this same person degraded you in front of all the people important to you? You know what your response *would* be; however, Jesus demonstrated what it *should* be.

What if it were not quite so dramatic? What if this offending person was deeply insecure and had some personality flaws that really got on your nerves? You know what your response *would* be; yet Jesus demonstrated what it *should* be.

What if this person had a lack of social graces that put him outside the "in-crowd"? You know what your response *would* be. Jesus demonstrated what it *should* be.

Do we love the "un-lovely"? Do we serve those ignored by the rest of the world? Do the disenfranchised have a franchise in our hearts?

May we become like Jesus who would have us lose our current response pattern and develop one like His.

The Way of Love

Love Is Serving

[He] rose from supper, . . . poured water into a basin and began to wash the disciples' feet, and to wipe them.   John 13:4, 5

In Jesus' demonstration, there is no room for vague misunderstanding of what love means. Love is an action of serving others. In the beginning of this chapter, it is noted that Jesus "loved His own who were in the world" to the end. In the next verses He demonstrates in practical terms what that love means.

If we are to love others and obey the commandment of our Lord, we are to serve one another.

We must lay down the garments of our own pride and of our own comfort, and we must pick up the towel of humility and service, looking for opportunities to actuate the call of our Lord to love (read "serve") one another.

Are you laying down the socio-spiritual status you "deserve" and accepting a place beneath that which you've earned? Are you serving?

Are you looking for opportunities to promote others—their well-being, their dreams, their programs, their agendas? Are you helping others and not just yourself? Are you serving? Are you loving?

The Way of Love

Dying to Self—Part 1

Greater love has no one than this, than to lay down one's life for his friends.
John 15:13

Laying down our lives for a friend—what does that mean? This passage can conjure up images of jumping in front of cars to save someone else or throwing ourselves in front of bullets intended for others. I don't think these were the images Jesus intended when He called us to love.

Perhaps laying down our lives for a friend means listening, really listening to others, even when it is not convenient.

Perhaps it means helping someone who does not give us strokes when we do it. Maybe it means turning off a ball game to have a tea party with a child. Perhaps it means forgoing our favorite chili-burger to stay healthier for our spouse's sake, and future.

It is much easier to muster a moment of nobility (as in throwing oneself in front of a bullet) than it is to lay down our lives for one another every day in small ways. We can only die for a friend once. But we can lay down our lives for a friend every day.

Dying to Self—Part 2

This is My commandment, that you love one another as I have loved you.   *John 15:12*

"How can I love as this passage requires? How am I to do it? It is not like I have not tried. I do. But I fail. How am I to love this way?"

We can love this way because we have an example. Jesus loved this way. He gave up the comfort, joy, and adoration of heaven to be with broken people and become dirtied by the soil of earth and the sin of humanity. He bore the agony of unjust pain as He faced Calvary and continued to give Himself for others. And He did this for love of you and me.

When we see His example, we are encouraged to bear the pain that broken people inflict upon us when we reach out to them. When their remarks stab us, when their rejection is cruel, when our love-actions earn us only scorn and hurt, we see Jesus. With Him as example, we are encouraged to continue to love and to keep on giving love in the face of pain.

If He did this for us, can we not do it for others?

The Way of Love

Dying to Self—Part 3

This is my commandment, that you love one another as I have loved you. Greater love has no one than this, than to lay down one's life for his friends.   *John 15:12, 13*

Again, how can I love as Jesus loved me? Even with the example Jesus sets before me, I find myself weak and unable to care for others as He does.

When the Scripture calls us to hold an attitude or behavior that seems impossible, our problem is that we feel that our willpower or discipline is required to make it happen. Perhaps it is the legacy of rugged individualism inherited from our ancestors who tamed a new continent, but it seems that the last place we go when we cannot love sacrificially is for help.

The whole walk of faith is one of going for help. If you cannot love as Jesus did, you must ask Him to reshape your being.

David asked the Lord to create a new and clean heart within him. This is the pathway to loving like Jesus. *He* creates the loving heart in us. Then perhaps we can love more like Him.

Choosing to Love

Giving all diligence, add to your faith virtue, to virtue knowledge . . . to godliness brotherly kindness, and to brotherly kindness love.
2 Peter 1:5, 7

In 2 Peter 1:3 Peter tells us how the power comes for us to live the life of "brotherly kindness." It comes as a gift, given to us by God Himself.

In verse 5, he exhorts us to operate with diligence as we add love to our faith. Here, it would seem that we should *work* toward Christ-like love.

Well, which is it? Is the capacity to love one another a gift, or is it a level we work toward? I think the answer is "yes."

Were it not for the grace-filled gift of character transformation and the sure and steady hand of our Lord upon our lives, we would be lost in sin, lost in self-absorption, and completely unable to love the selfless life to which Jesus calls us.

Yet, our Lord calls us to step out, to exercise our wills, and to begin to love. Then He comes in power to enable us to be like Him.

Whom will God enable us to love today?

The Way of Love

Koinonia—Part 1

*But if we walk in the light as He is in the light, we have fellow-
ship with one another.*   *1 John 1:7*

Koinonia is the word translated here "fellowship." If
we are walking in the light of our Lord, we have
koinonia with one another. So what does that word really
mean?

Two words are associated with *koinonia*. The disciples held
all property in common. A marketplace or a fountain was
the mutual property of the community. So this implies that
there is a mutuality, a common holding of resources, a
sharing of what we have together in our walk in the light of
our Lord.

Many of us feel that we have nothing of resource to offer
our brothers and sisters in Christ. Some also feel that our
brothers and sisters in Christ have nothing to offer us.
According to the Scripture, neither of these positions is
God's will for us.

If nothing else, we have the resource of a heart with which
to love, ears with which to listen, and hands with which to
care.

Are our resources being shared with others? Are their
resources being shared with us? Let us walk in the light
together. Let us have *koinonia*.

The Way of Love

Koinonia—Part 2

But if we walk in the light as He is in the light, we have fellow-ship with one another. 1 John 1:7

Besides a mutual sharing of resources implied in the word *koinonia,* there is also an implication of "pub-lic-ness." If we are to walk in the light of our Lord, there will be something of public-ness in our lives with one another. What does this mean?

Many of us are afraid to share what is inside our hearts for fear of being rejected. We fear "going public" with our weaknesses and failings. Our fellowship as believers and children of the light is supposed to dispel fear and allow us to be transparent, weak, vulnerable, and still be accepted by one another.

If there is anything John writes about, it is love. Our love for the Lord is the basis of our love for one another. And our love for one another is the basis of this ability to be transparent.

Are we loving? Are we reaching out? Are we living openly and transparent? Are we trustworthy enough to allow oth-ers to "go public"?

The Way of Love

Loving Through Hurt

For if you love [only] those who love you, what reward have you?
Matthew 5:46

A friend related that when she was growing up she had a black cat. She always named her cats by their color, but since she already had a black cat, when this one came along and had kittens, she called her "Mother-cat." Most cats are aloof and independent. But not Mother-cat. She would even jump into her lap when called. Mother-cat had the gentlest, kindest, and most endearing personality she had ever seen in a pet.

One morning my friend went out onto the patio to pet her. At a touch Mother-cat hissed, reached out, and scratched my friend. She got mad and yelled at the pet until Mother-cat limped away. She had been hit by a car the night before, and her hip was dislocated.

My friend told me the Lord impressed her that morning. It was as though He spoke and said, "You watch, young lady. You'll see people who snarl and scratch. But understand; they've been hurt. Look past the snarl and love the hurt."

She took Mother-cat to the vet. His loving touch healed her.

The Way of Love

Forgiveness

He who loves his brother abides in the light . . . but he who hates his brother . . . walks in darkness.   1 John 2:10, 11

*W*ebster defines hatred as a hostility, aversion, or dislike usually derived from fear, anger, or injury. This is exceedingly helpful as we look toward obeying our Lord's commandment to love.

Our fear makes us hate. Sometimes without true data-based confirmation, we feel someone does not like us. Our fear and anticipated rejection elicits aversion.

Our anger makes us hate. We have been wronged, legitimately wronged! "She injured me! I hate her!"

This is why faith and forgiveness are so important in God's value system. If we have faith, we do not give place to our unsubstantiated fears. If we have forgiveness, we don't entertain our anger or our hatred.

"But," you say, "those are easy platitudes; if only you understood the degree of injury, . . ."

If God calls us to love, there must be some provision for the really difficult-to-love cases. This provision is called forgiveness.

Do you hate somebody? Dislike? How about a slight aversion?

Lord, give us the capacity to forgive.

The Way of Love

Selfless or Selfish?

Now Jesus called His disciples to Himself and said, "I have compassion on the multitude."   Matthew 15:32

In a recent telethon one stand-up comic after another joined a big show for a relief project. In between each of the acts an announcer would address the television audience and ask for donations toward a worthy project.

One line from the show stood out. "Help those in need," the announcer said, "and feel good about yourself." The motivating factor behind helping those facing famine was selfish.

This pricks our conscience. Do we do good for others in order to feel holy, to feel important, to feel in control?

Jesus loves sacrificially. He commands us to love as He does. Love requires us to do good for others. Is our motivation selfless or selfish? If it is selfish, there is a good chance that our good deeds will be shallow and, more importantly, will not last.

Lord, make us like You. Cause our love to be lasting in its effect.

Love Takes Work

Love suffers long. 1 Corinthians 13:4

In his book *The Four Loves,* C. S. Lewis compares our God-given human capacity to love to a garden. "[Such] a garden," he says, "will not fence and weed itself, nor prune its own fruit trees, nor roll and cut its own lawns. It will remain a garden, as distinct from a wilderness, only if someone does all these things to it. [Although] it needs constant weeding and pruning . . . it teems with life. It glows with color and smells like heaven and puts forward at every hour of a summer day beauties which man could never have created and could not even, on his own resources, have imagined."

Because we were created in the image of God, we have a natural capacity to love one another. Because we live in a fallen world, we have to work at loving the many kinds of personalities living within our sphere.

Love takes discipline, practice, and work. But if we will exert our directed energy, we will enjoy blessings we could never have imagined.

Take a moment to look at your "garden" today. How is it coming along?

The Way of Love

Kind Confrontation

Love . . . is kind.   *1 Corinthians 13:4*

The infant daughter was just becoming mobile. Her crawling was transitioning to walking, and her walking had taken her to the hallway furnace. She was aware that the heater was cool to the touch, but with knowledge of the coming winter, mommy and daddy patiently instructed her of the "no-touch" quality of the furnace.

The story is an old one. The first hand swat was infinitely more painful for daddy than for daughter. Sometimes love, in its kindness, must confront.

When we talk of the confrontational side of love, some jump on the bandwagon. "Tough love," "drill sergeant," "don't spare the rod"; these words resonate in their souls. But often the "tough" is there without the kindness of love.

Others shrink away from confrontational love. "Tenderness," "tolerance," "forbearance"; these are their words.

Yet we know that the picture of loving community in the Scripture is a balance.

Are we honest in our dealings with those God has called us to love? Honest enough to confront? Tender in doing it?

The Way of Love

Solitude

For by one Spirit we were all baptized into one body.
1 Corinthians 12:13

To live in harmony with one another requires intro-spection. What keeps us from functioning as a body with our brothers and sisters? Pride? The baggage of past relational hurts? What keeps us distant from the very ones who will bring health and fulfillment to us?

In order to assess these internal issues, we must have a time of solitude, a time to hear from God. In his book on Christian community, *Life Together,* Deitrich Bonhoeffer devotes two chapters to the pursuit of body life. He entitles them "The Day Together" and "The Day Alone." In order to live, love, and operate together, we must take time to be alone.

Solitude gives us time to hear God as He probes our souls to convict us of sinful attitudes toward one another. Solitude gives us time to hear God speak to us about our points of brokenness which handicap us from fulfilling community.

As we move toward community, we must also learn to be alone. We need the re-creating stillness of solitude with our Lord if we are to be with others meaningfully.

The Way of Love

Unity

Keep the unity of the Spirit in the bond of peace.   *Ephesians 4:3*

Loneliness is one of the primary sorrows of our fragmented and disjointed society today. We all feel it at some time. We may even be overwhelmed and immobilized by its destructive effects.

Our Lord, who designed us, never intended us to be alone. We were intended to live in community with one another. And He provided a lifestyle which, if embraced, eliminates the power of loneliness.

Yet our fear of loneliness causes us to move with herd mentality—following the masses, flowing with the tide of societal and cultural dictates. The fear of loneliness often generates personal compromise of our spiritual, ethical, and moral dreams and aspirations. We want to follow Jesus with all our strength, but we fear isolation and alone-ness as we move against the tide.

To attend us on our "against-the-tide" way, our Lord calls us to caring, loving unity with His children. If we will walk in the unity of the Spirit as our Lord enjoins, our obedience will remove the sting of isolation from our lives.

Reconciliation

We came to your brother Esau, and he also is coming to meet you, and four hundred men are with him.　　　　*Genesis 32:6*

houghtless or sinful actions so easily create a rift between us and those Jesus commands us to love. Reconciliation is so awkward. We hate to admit our own sinfulness. We hate to admit our own stupidity. We hate to make the first move.

Jacob can give us courage at times like these. He alienated Esau by being a liar and a crook, and now it was time to be reconciled. For him it was not just embarrassment that kept him from taking the first step. Esau was coming at him with four hundred warriors. There was a good chance that death would be the outcome of this reconciliation attempt. He had more to worry about than personal prestige or honor.

To take the first step in reconciliation takes courage, bravery, strength, and character. For Jacob it took more. He had to be willing to abandon his life in order to obey the Lord and be reconciled.

Let each of us, today, be as willing as Jacob to set aside everything for reconciliation.

The Way of Love

Learning to Yield—Part 1

. . . you shall fall down and worship the gold image that King Nebuchadnezzar has set up.   Daniel 3:5

Nebuchadnezzar felt that his kingdom was threatened. Loss of unity in the kingdom seemed to threaten all that he had conquered and acquired. In a dream the Lord had warned him of imminent loss if he did not yield to His rulership. Being resourceful however, Nebuchadnezzar devised a plan to consolidate his holdings by uniting the people around a single religion centering around a great golden image of Nebuchadnezzar himself.

How often do we operate with the same mindset? We feel a need; we have a fear. A relationship is slipping away, and we need a friend. We are alone. What do we do?

So often we clutch. Our fear of isolation or loss often elicits a desperate clutching response in our relationships.

God *wants* fulfilling relationships for us, not gained through manipulation or clutching, but through yieldedness to His ways, His plans for our lives, and His Word.

In our relationships are we clutching or yielding?

The Way of Love

Learning to Yield—Part 2

Our God . . . is able to deliver us . . . but if not, . . . [we will not]
worship the gold image. Daniel 3:17, 18

In contrast to Nebuchadnezzar, who was clutching after what God had warned him he could not keep if he did not change, these young Hebrews demonstrated the "yieldedness" to God's purpose for them. They were willing to give up careers, friendships, and lives to follow their Lord. In this yieldedness, we see the Lord fulfill their needs.

In our relationships with one another, we often grab and clutch to see our own needs met. In contrast, we see these young men guide us down the pathway to fulfilling relationships—they were not only a strength to one another as they stood for what they believed, but they saw the Lord confirm His relationship with them as He moved into their situation.

The Lord knows how much we need to be united with others; He created us that way. Rather than clutching, however, we need to let go.

If you will seek the kingdom of God first, if you will yield all you have to His purposes, He has promised to meet all your needs, including your relational needs.

The Way of Love

Confession

He who covers his sins will not prosper, but whoever confesses and forsakes them will have mercy.   *Proverbs 28:13*

So often we wish to present our best side, to put our best foot forward. This may be a good thing to do in a job interview, but it is not a good operating principle for Christian community. If we cover our failures and keep them from one another, we live a pretense. If we refuse to allow one another to see who we really are, "warts and all," there can be no support, no encouragement, no account- ability, and no forgiveness.

We may feel that confessing our flaws, our sins, and our shortcomings to the Lord is good enough. It is good, but Scripture challenges us to take the extra step toward trans- parency by confessing our faults to one another (James 5:16).

We are fooling ourselves to believe that we are free from tragic flaws. Only when we live in honest, burden-bearing fellowship with one another do we see what our worst flaws are. In this environment we have a loving community to help us see our sin and brokenness, and also to direct us toward wholeness.

Forgiveness

Joseph said to his brothers, . . . "I am Joseph your brother, whom you sold into Egypt."

Genesis 45:4

The story of Joseph is an early account of the forgiving nature God expects us to display in our treatment of those who have wronged us. It is a prime example of Christ-like love. Though Joseph's brothers sold him into slavery and deceived his father into thinking him dead, when he confronts his brothers during their time of need, forgiveness and love burst forth from his heart.

With uncanny faith in the overriding providence of God, Joseph even professes his belief that God had redeemed his brothers' betrayal of him by using it as a means to deliver his family during the time of famine. Joseph's forgiveness of his brothers' sin is so complete that he kisses each of them and weeps with joy at being united with them once again.

Brotherly forgiveness is expressive, self-giving, and offered in a way that is easily received. Today, let us be alert to an opportunity to show the same kind of love and forgiveness that Joseph did to someone that God may bring across our path.

The Way of Love

Emotional Healing

Love has been perfected among us in this . . . because as He is, so are we in this world.   *1 John 4:17*

In the book *Great Expectations*, Charles Dickens paints a picture of love broken, twisted, and then reproduced. Elderly Miss Haversham had been the victim of great cruelty. At the cunning and revengeful hand of her scorned brother, her fiancé left her at the altar on her wedding day. Her brokenness showed for a lifetime in her loneliness, her bitterness, her anger, and her caustic personality. More sorrowful yet was the reproduction of her unloving traits in the innocent child Estella she so profoundly influenced.

We, too, affect the lives and attitudes of those around us. If we allow past hurt to keep us from loving, we will suffer. But we will not suffer alone. Our actions *will* influence those around us. They *will* be reproduced in the lives of others.

But Jesus heals. If you are paralyzed and unable to love, Jesus heals. Every past hurt forgiven and presented to our Lord frees the fresh water of His love to flow through us. We experience the joy of love around us, and those we influence enjoy its benefits in their own lives.

The Way of Love

Confession

Confess your trespasses to one another, and pray for one another, that you may be healed.   *James 5:16*

Ours is a nation founded on the expansive and isolating frontier. Our culture springs from rugged individualism and is directly opposed to the principle of interdependence necessary for Christian community.

Yet living in true Christian community requires vulnerability and honesty with one another. It requires honest evaluation of our own sinfulness, weakness, and character flaws. It requires that, having admitted these, we share them with the embracing community of fellow-saints who have their own weaknesses.

We fear that confession of failure makes us weak. We fear that vulnerability exposes us to onslaught.

While it is true that vulnerability exposes us, if it is in the context of the love Jesus commanded us to bear for one another, it is an exposure for the better. It can be like the exposure we allow to a surgeon. In actuality, confession makes us whole and strong. It takes courage and initiative, but it returns a dividend of greater strength, greater courage, clearer character, and enhanced godlikeness.

The Way of Love

March

The Kingdom of God

Kingdom Renewal

Come, let us go to Gilgal and renew the kingdom there.

1 Samuel 11:14

The phrase "the Kingdom of God" is more than familiar; it has almost become shopworn. Still, these words at the heart of Jesus' preaching deserve to be the best understood in all our minds. We need to grasp their fullness, weight and dimension.

There is a worldwide spiritual renewal in progress throughout the Church today.

Wherever it is occurring, a richer understanding of the kingdom seems to be related to this renewal. What "new" or "renewing" of *kingdom truth* do I need to hear and receive?

1 Samuel 11 tells a story of a vicious monarch's effort at gouging out the eyes of every individual in an ancient village of Israel. In response, Saul, their newly crowned leader, rises to smash Nahash, the arrogant enemy who proposed the blinding torture. As a result, the whole population of Israel *saw; saw* not only by reason of their vision having been spared, but *saw* the beauty and power of Saul, their God-given king!

Samuel's call, "Come . . . let us renew the kingdom," may well be heard by all of us today. As our adversary the devil seeks to blind us to the glories and the power of Jesus Himself, let us instead *"Come* and be renewed in our understanding of Him—His kingdom's power and glory."

Kingdom of God

Kingdom Glory

For my eyes have seen the King, the Lord of hosts.   Isaiah 6:5

To capture a vision of the heart of *kingdom truth* is to catch the vision of the *King Himself!* All understanding of "the kingdom of God" begins, develops and climaxes in knowing—in *seeing* Jesus. "Let us *know,* let us *pursue* the knowledge of the Lord," Hosea cried; while Paul declares, ". . . that I may know *Him!*" (Hos. 6:3; Phil. 3:10).

Isaiah had come to his place of devotions one day, just as we have. He describes the nature of the times: "In the year that King Uzziah died . . . *I saw the Lord!*" (Is. 6:1). There is something powerfully instructive in his testimony, for we are shown the transient, changing, decaying rule of dying man contrasted with the steadfast, glorious rule of the Living God.

In the same way, the Holy Spirit's awakening us to the beauty of the message of "the kingdom of God" comes at a time when world kingdoms are in a bewildering state of flux. These upheavals have a way of shaking the foundations of everything around us—family, job, personal security. But as Isaiah, let's turn our *hearts* toward Him, hungry for the King Himself. See *Him,* the Source of kingdom life, hope and glory . . . Today!

Kingdom Prayer—Part 1

Your kingdom come, your will be done.   *Luke 11:2*

C. S. Lewis said, "There are only two kinds of people: those who say to God, 'Thy will be done;' and those to whom God ultimately says, '*Thy* will be done.'" How startling it is to weigh the implications of our *seeking* and *surrendering* to the rule of God in our hearts. To *invite* His kingly reign is to receive its forgiving, freeing and ennobling purposes for each of our lives. To *ignore* Him assures our self-rule, and thereby its pitiful, painful, and destructive results.

Kingdom praying begins to find its power when we have come to the place of clear priority: "*Your* kingdom come!" It's often difficult to come to God's throne without my own "wish list"—my personal agenda of how I think things ought to be, and whom I think God ought to change to suit my tastes. But true kingdom praying comes to its highest possibility when I bow my lowest in surrender. "Lord, *You* help me think *Your* thoughts about the circumstances and the people surrounding me—and let me serve *Your* purposes in this present world. Your kingdom come *here* at my small spot on earth—as You will it in heaven. Amen."

Kingdom of God

Kingdom Prayer—Part 2

Your kingdom come . . . on earth.   *Luke 11:2*

We cannot leave the matter of kingdom praying without being clear about its pivotal place in the affairs of this world. Jesus' lesson on prayer, which we call the Lord's Prayer, not only issues a call to our worship and surrender before God's throne—to submission. He also issues an incredible directive, an assignment that we accept a decisive role as intercessors. In short, our intervention in prayer, calling "Your kingdom come," is that action which refuses to surrender this present world to the adversary's devices and destruction.

In WWII artillery firepower from giant guns situated miles away was directed by advance "spotters." These military personnel were in a position to see the target, then to radio the position where needed firepower could be directed to destroy the enemy's encampments.

This is the same as Jesus' assignment that we pray, "Father, Your kingdom come *on earth.*" It is our Savior's way of saying, "Just as you have welcomed the Father's rule in your hearts, now *extend* that kingdom rule in prayer." Point to earth's needy places and invite heaven's forces to break hell's strongholds and bring hearts, homes and nations into His freedom.

Kingdom of God

Kingdom Joy

The kingdom of God is . . . righteousness and peace and joy in the Holy Spirit.   Romans 14:17

No human systems can generate the dimensions of fullness and fulfillment God's *kingdom life* bring us. The present passion so many of us feel, to drink of "all the fullness of God," is a quest for the way the Holy Spirit glorifies Jesus as King in our daily life and living. There are no religious substitutes for the reality of this order of life.

As Paul wrote here, he was laboring with a problem, for everywhere he turned he found opponents to the message of Christ's kingdom joys. His most ardent enemies weren't Roman soldiers or the Roman government, but a strange breed of religious diehards. They knew the true God but hated the refreshing liberty of Holy Spirit-filled living Paul was preaching. They kept imposing ritual requirements related to the Mosaic code—issues concerning certain "eating and drinking" stipulations. Paul wasn't arguing for undisciplined living but simply for unsaddled souls! In effect, he says, "God's kingdom isn't in the trappings of tradition, but His rule brings His *right* ways (righteousness), His *mighty* ways (peace) and His *bright* ways (joy)." Let's *all* open fully to such fullness—and to His kingdom's expansion in our souls.

Kingdom of God

The King's Pleasure

Do not fear, little flock.   Luke 12:32

Such awesome privileges and responsibilities in our being assigned so pivotal a role as determining *where* God's kingdom power shall "invade" this world can almost seem frightening. You may think, "Who am I to lay claim to such power?" But Jesus has anticipated our reluctance and feelings of unworthiness. He says, "Don't be afraid—it is the Father's will to give you the kingdom."

There is a tender significance in the Greek verb form used here. Our text might well be freely translated: "It is the Father's delight to press the kingdom into your childlike hands." It's a beautiful verbal picture our Savior paints for us. Imagine little children today leaving for school. A charitable fund has invited contributions from each home, so the father takes money and ties it in a handkerchief. Then, he presses it into the child's hand and ties the gift and the kerchief to his or her wrist. *Now* it is certain. The father's desire to make the gift will find its destination via his child's hand. And so Jesus says, "Don't be afraid to receive prayer's powerful potential to change your world. It's the Father's loving gift—through you!"

Kingdom Keys—Part 1

And I will give you the keys of the kingdom of heaven.

Matthew 16:19

Keys represent privilege, trust and authority. When a teenager receives the keys to the family car, a distinct turning point has been reached. Growth, preparedness, training and trust converge in the release of this expensive vehicle unto the care and use of a son or daughter. It's a big day, but also a weighty moment, for the authority being granted could be as destructive as it is beneficial. Is the child ready?

When Jesus said He would give His disciples "the keys of the kingdom of heaven," He based it on each one's coming to the same place of understanding Peter had reached when he said, "You are the Christ, the Son of the living God" (v. 16). In other words, "the keys" are given to people who fully recognize Jesus as their King, and who yield to His rule as the mandate for their own lives. It is *then* that He says, "Now I am transmitting to you a representative role."

As keys give access, He opens a new arena of possibility for us. As keys verify trust, He entrusts arenas of service to us. And just as keys *ignite, lock* and *loose,* Christ sends us to people and circumstances waiting to be 'turned on,' 'closed in' and 'set free.' Let's keep learning about these keys.

Kingdom of God

Kingdom Keys—Part 2

Since that time the kingdom of God has been preached and every-one is pressing into it.   Luke 16:16

On this occasion Jesus answered the questions of critics who decried His generosity with former sinners. His readiness to forgive and lift the fallen to places of new possibilities infuriated them. He referred them to an era; a new time which began with John the Baptist's call to "Repent, for the kingdom of heaven is at hand!" (Matt. 3:2). Jesus went on to say that from that time forward—*and to this day*—people who choose God's rule for their lives press into it. The figure of speech is one which indicates earnestness and urgency.

Entering into the dimension of God's life and grace isn't a casual matter. In likening this "entry" to the travail of birth (John 3:3), Jesus is emphasizing our full attention and commitment.

The "keys of the kingdom," that is, *access to* and *functioning in* the kingdom, are capacities promised to everyone who calls Jesus *Lord.* As we submit to His rule in our lives, with characteristic grace and generosity, He responds by fully sharing His power and His authority with us. It's an overwhelming concept: His sovereign power invites our partnership as joint-heirs with Him (Rom. 8:16, 17). Let's keep growing in this grace!

Kingdom of God

Kingdom Keys—Part 3

For indeed, the kingdom of God is within you. — Luke 17:20

There is an international law concerning ambassadors of foreign kingdoms, that wherever that individual may be authorized as a full representative of his government, he cannot be arrested. It is the law of "diplomatic immunity," and in essence it says, "Where this person stands—even on foreign soil—he stands in his *own* land!"

In much the same way, Jesus taught us concerning the presence and power of God's kingdom in our own lives. Once we have been "born again" and *birthed as citizens* into the Father's family and kingdom royalty, we can live immune to the control of the evil powers of darkness who would seek to confine God's purposes in us.

When Jesus said, "The kingdom of God is within you," He was declaring a point we are wise to embrace with understanding. He was *not* suggesting we have become self-serving gods, nor was He proposing some humanistic mind-science. But He *was*—and *is saying,* "The Father's ruling might is now within you. It is not distant nor is it unavailable. Take the 'keys' I've placed in your hands—faith, hope, love, joy, peace, life, strength, healing—and *apply them.*" In short, as ambassadors, we are assigned to spread the life of the kingdom wherever we go.

Kingdom of God

Kingdom Keys—Part 4

And whatever you bind on earth will be bound in heaven.
Matthew 16:19

One pastor explained the phenomenal gift which Jesus has made to us of "the keys of the kingdom of God" in this way: "I have on my key ring," he began, "a selection of keys which are very deterministic. One determines who can enter my house, another who can drive my car, and another who can access my office and business matters. Each of these keys is shared by different people. My children have keys to my house, my oldest daughter has a key to my car, and my secretary and associates have a key to my office. However, there is only *one* person who has an *equal* set of keys to mine; only one person with whom I share everything in common trust, and that is my wife.

"In the same way," he continued, "our Lord Jesus has spoken to us, the ones He calls His 'bride'. Because you are My own, My redeemed, My beloved and My trusted ones—I want you to have a full and equal share in everything that is Mine."

So it is, Jesus says, "You decide what of evil is *stopped* (bound) on earth, and you decide what of God's power and grace is released (loosed) to mankind." His "keys" have been entrusted to us—His redeemed Bride.

Kingdom of God

Kingdom People

He has . . . conveyed us into the kingdom of the Son of His love.
Colossians 1:13

There is no more dramatic word than "birth," the word Jesus used to describe the radical "delivery" of our life from sin into God's kingdom (John 3:3, 5). But almost matching that dynamic metaphor is Paul's saying, "He has *conveyed* us into the kingdom." This word was used when ancient kings took captive peoples and transported them to another land, usually as slaves.

But here, we as *former* slaves now taken captive by our Savior King are being transported from former bondage in sin to the liberated atmosphere of His daily presence. "Therefore, if the Son makes you free, you shall be free indeed" (John 8:36).

While our ultimate "transporting" will be into His presence at His coming, in the meantime He has not left us at the mercy of the "dark rulers" of this present age (1 John 5:19; Eph. 6:12). We are His people, proclaiming His praises (1 Pet. 2:9), showing His good works (Matt. 5:16) and holding forth His Word (Phil. 2:15, 16). We have come under the rule of our supreme King who also is the Lover of our souls; who has "conveyed" us unto His kingdom to serve kingdom enterprises.

Kingdom of God

Kingdom Enterprise

Do business till I come.   *Luke 19:13*

Jesus likened this present era during which we await His return as a season of time His people are to be "doing business." He illustrated this as a heavenly investment program by which He distributes to us the wealth of His life, love and grace. He then assigns us to "operate"— to do business in His Name until He returns. (Someone has suggested the corporation's name is "God and Sons, Inc."!)

The New Testament word translated "do business" is the one from which we have derived our English word "pragmatic." Noticing that can intensify our awareness that *spiritual* living is not ethereal, escapist or other-wordly. It is right-smack-dab-in-the-middle-of-reality—here and now.

Today, invite the Holy Spirit to make you aware of "kingdom moments of opportunity"—situations in which you can do business, or "conduct trade." Many people need to meet someone who can "trade" kingdom resources for their human need; who will trade *love* for the fear that binds them, *healing* for the sickness that afflicts them, *forgiveness* for the sin that stains them, *strength* for the weakness they feel. Today, let us conduct kingdom enterprise, "doing business" in Jesus' Name.

Kingdom of God

Kingdom Mysteries—Part 1

It has been given to you to know the mysteries of the kingdom.
Matthew 13:11

The Bible word "mystery" is almost a mystery in its own right, because its meaning has reversed. When Jesus used it, it meant "a former secret now openly told." Today, it refers to something difficult to grasp, understand or figure out.

It's important for us to understand this because Jesus is *clearly* wanting to make His purposes *clear to us*. There's nothing mysterious about what He's wanting to say, to do or to bring about . . . , that is, IF.

The one qualification to understanding God's way for you today or His will for your whole life is to *listen*. The parable of the seed and the soil (Matt. 13:2–9) precedes His promise to unfold "kingdom mysteries" to us. Its message is unmistakable: You must have 'ears to hear' (v. 9). Only then do we gain insight, understanding and growth in fruitfulness (v. 12).

In this light, let us begin every day, praying words such as those so beautifully sung in this worship chorus: "Open our ears, Lord, and help us to listen, open our eyes, Lord, we want to see Jesus."

Kingdom of God

Kingdom Mysteries—Part 2

Blessed are your eyes for they see, and your ears for they hear.
Matthew 13:16

Deafness and blindness are problems that afflict our entire race, not merely those with recognizable physical handicaps. In fact, it is often the case that the physically impaired person "sees" and "hears" better than those of us having our hearing and eyesight. The testimony to our spiritually and attitudinally blind-and-deaf condition is demonstrated in the frequency we will hear people say, "I don't *see* how they could do that to me," or, "I just won't *hear* of it!"

So much of the time we humans neither *see* the need and pain or *hear* the heartcry and ache of those around us. We tend only to react out of our own frustration, when instead our Savior is seeking to cultivate our "listening" and "seeing" skills so we can *serve* human need rather than seeking to be served.

Jesus pronounced the blessing we read above because His disciples were experiencing the fulfillment of God's age-long objective (v. 17). As His "once-hidden-now-revealed" purposes have been shown to us in Christ, let us remember: Seeing and hearing Him will make us *more* "seeing" and "hearing" toward others.

Kingdom of God

Kingdom Growth

For the earth yields crops . . . the blade . . . the head . . . the full grain.
Mark 4:28

The poster read, "Lord, please give me patience; and give it to me NOW!" How like us all! And the same trait seems all the more tempting as we begin to learn of our privileges as people of the kingdom. Since our Lord has commissioned us to "Go and bring forth fruit," it is understandable that as we pray, or as we do kingdom business, that we would prefer quick or immediate *action*.

But Jesus is reminding us of how "kingdom growth" occurs. As *surely* as it is true that the words we speak in prayer *are* heard, and as *surely* as the promises of God we claim are seed, so just as certainly it takes time for those promises sown in prayer to come to fruition.

The parallel is beautiful: we sow as God's Word is laid hold of in faith; we water with prayer and praise; His love and grace provide the sunshine—and the fruitfulness of harvest will come! But remember the process: first, the small, grassy blade of mere beginnings; second, the growing evidence of coming fruit; and finally, the fulfilled promise in its completeness.

Kingdom of God

Kingdom Balance

*The kingdom of heaven is at hand . . . the harvest is the end of
the age.* Matthew 4:17; 13:24, 39

Life in Christ is lived in a marvelously wonderful
tension between points of balanced understanding.
For example: We *are* saved (from sin's penalty, death), and
we are *being* saved (from the efforts of sin to rule our flesh)
and we *will be* saved (from the presence of sin) at Jesus'
Coming. This progression is crucial to understanding life
in Christ. Another essential balance point is seeing that
God's kingdom power is present *now,* and that yet it still
will not be fully present until *then*—when Jesus comes.

Learning to live with both a holy boldness in faith and an
appropriate humility in patience is a grace few seem to
learn. In Matthew 13, the same One who said, "The power
of God's kingdom is *right here, right now*" (Matt. 4), gives a
series of parables which show three things. *First,* there are
immediate things that happen when God's rule is welcomed and received *now. Second,* there are many things
that faith sets in motion, but which take time to conclude.
And *third,* there are some aspects of Christ's ultimate kingdom dominion that will not be manifest until "the end of
the age." Let us pray today: "Lord, make me bold to expect
what is for *now* and patient to wait for what is yet in the
future."

Kingdom of God

Kingdom Character—Part 1

Blessed are the poor in spirit. Matthew 5:3

The kingdom of God is not a distant realm. When Jesus spoke of "the kingdom of heaven," He was not talking about a city in the sky or about church on Sunday. He was talking about God's rule as it bears on our lives today. The "kingdom" is a *realm* (it occurs in the invisible realm, in human hearts) and a *rule* (it operates by the power of God).

G. Campbell Morgan, the great Bible expositor of the early 20th century, called Jesus' Sermon on the Mount, "The Manifesto of The Kingdom." Our text for today opens that "manifesto"—His proclamation of the kingdom lifestyle He intended to bring about in those who submit to God's rule in their lives. The first character trait Jesus mentions of people who receive the kingdom could be misinterpreted as becoming "pitiful or self-pitying." But rather, to be "poor in spirit" means to be humbly dependent on God and God alone.

Just as "poor in resources" causes a person to admit, "I don't have what it takes and I can't gain it on my own"; so, we acknowledge ourselves as "kingdom people" when we say: "Father, *only You* have what I need, and I depend upon You alone to show Your way in Your time."

Kingdom of God

Kingdom Character—Part 2

*Whoever does and teaches (God's commandments), he shall be
called great in the kingdom of heaven.*   *Matthew 5:19*

Here is a remarkable truth worthy of our fullest
understanding. Because of the fact that we are
"saved by grace" and without "the works of the Law" (Eph.
2:8, 9; Gal. 2:16), some misapply these words of Jesus. He
notes that while our salvation is neither based on nor sustained by our performance of the Law of God's Old
Testament commandments, we are still called to obey
them.

In describing the character traits of kingdom people, Jesus
emphasizes this. He was unmistakably clear: People who
teach that God's Old Testament Law is unimportant are
"least" in His value system; people who *do* and *teach* the
Law are "great." Of course, this is not intended to induce a
guilty sense of failure for Laws we disobey. Neither is it to
bring defeat to our souls when we are still "learning to
walk," and sometimes stumble over God's commandments.
Our salvation is secured in Christ's Cross, and our justification insures our continuing acceptance with God. But
still, as we grow and go forward in the life of the kingdom,
the commandments of God provide a holy blueprint for
successful, liberated living.

Thank God, He has given the Holy Spirit to enable us to
live above condemnation and in growing obedience to the
Law! (Rom. 8:1–39).

Kingdom of God

Kingdom Character—Part 3

But seek first the kingdom of God. Matthew 6:33

There are perhaps no more reassuring words in the Bible which evidence God's personal, protective and provisioning care for each of us than those spoken by our Lord Jesus. In Matthew 6:25–34 He so clearly links us with the Father's heart for *all* His creation that we see two lessons at once.

First, creation itself has not been surrendered to mere self-perpetuating care. God has invested something of His own self in His creation, in the same way artists or crafts-men pour their skills—and thereby their fullest interest—into their work.

Second, humankind are the peak of the Father's creative masterwork; endowed uniquely with His image and pos-sessed of rare potential both temporal and eternal. No wonder He cares as He does! And therefore, Jesus affirms to us: The Father won't overlook your need, so *don't worry!*

But in this context our Lord does tell us what we are to concern ourselves with. He says, *Do seek* the interests of God's Kingdom! *Do* love. *Do* serve. *Do* help the fallen. *Do* reach out with salvation's power and grace. Our appointed schedule of priorities is established: *"You* take first interest in the things that concern My desire to reach, touch and love others, and *I'll* take care of everything that concerns you."

Kingdom of God

Kingdom Character—Part 4

Not everyone who says to Me, 'Lord, Lord,' shall enter the king-
dom.   *Matthew 7:21*

Jesus' manifesto of the lifestyle of God's kingdom people in the Sermon on the Mount (Matt. 5—7) concludes with a startling disclosure and a stunning illustration. The illustration is a contrast between a house that
stands solidly against hurricane force winds, and one that
is in shambles in the wake of the gale. Christ's summary of
the two is terse: The one which stood characterizes the person who hears and does what He commands, while the one
that was ruined demonstrates the life which considers obedience as an option, not a requirement. The ruin of the lat-
ter and the steadfastness of the former are graphic in their
message to us. Everything about our lives will rise or fall
depending upon our obedience to His ways.

But an even greater issue appears. We have a future
accounting also. On the one hand, Jesus relates the
promise and reward of those who walk with Him in faithful service. One day, He will personally greet us with His
"Well done!" (Matt. 25:21, 23). But inescapably present is
the solemn reminder of today's text. Appearances and
words without commitment and obedience receive His
final rejection. So today—tomorrow and ever—let us walk
as kingdom people who obey Him as Lord, as well as who
claim Him as Savior.

Kingdom of God

Kingdom Prototype—Part 1

What then shall we say that Abraham our father has found . . . ?
Romans 4:1

When a jet aircraft thunders down the runway and rises majestically to soar like an arrow to its destination, we are reminded of the accomplishments of human engineering. But we might also be reminded that not one of those was built without conformity to the prototype—the original form, pattern or model after which the whole fleet is designed. This wisdom in engineering is founded upon the most practical of principles: only build upon patterns that work!

In the "kingdom" order of things, Abraham has been declared the "father" of all who have chosen to walk by faith in obedience to Jesus Christ, God's Son. Accordingly, Romans 4 shows Abraham as a prototype—the "first of a line," which God planned (or "engineered" the design) would soar to higher destinies than fallen man or fleshly motivated humans could ever reach.

We are not told of Abraham's beginning here (as one who trusts in God's grace to save, not his own works—v. 2–4), but pointed toward a study of his life. This is a handbook on "kingdom living," charted through one man's lessons in faith centuries before Christ. It merits our turning to Genesis 12, where God began with Abraham. From his initial call to faith, we are taught in practical, prototypical terms: the "faith engineered" life will fly!

Kingdom of God

Kingdom Prototype—Part 2

I will bless you and make your name great and you shall be a blessing.   *Genesis 12:2*

The New Testament so explicitly directs us to "walk in the steps of the faith which our father Abraham had," that it's a matter of basic discipleship to examine his life in the Old Testament. In the Scriptures, the Holy Spirit shows Abraham as more than merely a study of history— he's a study in prophecy! Abraham's life is a forecast of (1) the *kind* of things people of Christ's kingdom will face, and (2) the *ways* by which they can triumph through faith.

At the outset, God announces a twofold objective: "I want to make your name great," and "You shall be a blessing." God's promise to make Abraham's name great was not a promise of fame, but a guarantee He would shape great character in him.

The biblical concept of "fame" focuses on the quality of the person's trustworthiness, integrity and spiritual weight. That's important to remember, since today we live in a society which mocks its own habit for "making people famous for nothing more than merely being well known." Thus fame today may be acquired through scandal as quickly as through accomplishment. Either may make the cover of *People* magazine!

But Abraham's *name* became great through learning a walk of worship and a pathway of persistent pursuit of God's will. That's kingdom character! It's the path to which the prototype calls us.

Kingdom of God

Kingdom Prototype—Part 3

And there he built an altar to the Lord.   Genesis 12:7

Above all other traits, kingdom people are people of worship. This means you will find them assembling with fellow believers in worship on the Lord's Day (Heb. 10:25). With and beyond that, you will also find their daily lives marked by a trail of altars . . . much as Abraham's was.

To study Abraham as the prototype personality who "fathered" a pathway of faith ages ago (Rom. 4:25) is to discover a life punctuated by altars—times of life-transforming encounters with God. (See Genesis 12:7, 8; 13:4, 18; 15:1–18; 21:1–19.) From episodes wherein he seals God's promises to him by building and bowing at an altar of worship, to instances where he sacrifices his all before God as an expression of his utmost trust, the *prototype pathway* for a kingdom walk in worship is mapped with clarity.

God's high calling to all of us is according to the same promise He made to Abraham: "I will bless you, and you will be a blessing." As staggering as that prospect may seem—that God could make us such a blessing—He is able to fulfill it as we walk before Him in "altar-building" worship.

Kingdom of God

Kingdom Territory

*Having disarmed principalities and power . . . triumphing over
them in it.*   *Colossians 2:15*

The "it" Paul's words in our text refer to is the cross.
The cross of Christ is the sole instrument for humanity's salvation and deliverance and the sole power for
breaking hell's works and operations. First Corinthians 2:7,
8 confirms this truth, showing how God's wisdom through
the blood and death of His Son completely confounded the
strategies of hell. They have never recovered, nor will they
ever recover!

These words are such a holy and healthy reminder to all of
us who want and welcome the fullness of the Holy Spirit to
make Christ's kingdom power effective in and through our
lives today. They point to the *place* from which "all power"
flows. For just as Jesus is the *Person* to whom, through
whom and from whom all God's power flows, so His cross
is the *place*—the foundational accomplishment which
releases all power to all mankind.

This is holy territory. It's where salvation's price was paid
and where sin's penalty was broken. The cross is also where
hell was "made a spectacle of," and "it"—the cross—has
become the sign by which we conquer. As the old hymn
asks, "Are you living in the shadow of the Cross?" Let's
answer, "Amen!"

Kingdom of God

Kingdom Priests—Part 1

And you shall be to me a kingdom of priests, a holy nation.

Exodus 19:6

The miracle-laden story of Israel's deliverance from Egyptian bondage is the pivotal event of the Old Testament. Its sum and substance is a God-intended forecast, inscribed in His eternal Word to teach us today—by type and by example (1 Cor. 10:11). The beginning point, their deliverance through the blood of the passover lamb, is the most precious and most obvious lesson, one which is fulfilled in us when we receive Christ as our Passover Lamb—as Savior and as our Deliverer (John 1:29; 1 Cor. 5:7).

As we follow this divinely ordained pattern for new life in the "kingdom-of-the-freed," there is a specific purpose to which we are called: to be a kingdom of priests. It is in pursuing this path that all God's purposes in us will be fulfilled and victorious living realized. This path is *the priestly pathway of worship.*

In God's words to Moses, which we read above, let us see the changelessness of this priestly call. *They* were called to a ministry of worship, precisely the same as that to which we are called (Rev. 1:5, 6). To answer this call, let us invite the Holy Spirit freshly to fill us for this ministry of worship.

Kingdom of God

Kingdom Priests—Part 2

*But you are a chosen generation, a royal priesthood, a holy
nation.*   *1 Peter 2:9*

After Israel was delivered from Egypt, God's original
plan was that *all the nation* would be a priesthood.
The sad fact is that because of sin only one tribe—Levi—
finally became the priestly people (Exodus 32). God's
desire to free an entire nation to be priestly ministers to the
whole world was never realized (Ex. 19:5–7).

However, in Christ and under the new covenant, this
objective is within the scope of fulfillment. Peter writes,
"You are . . . a holy priesthood to offer up spiritual sacrifices acceptable to God through Jesus Christ" (1 Pet. 2:5).
These words provide one of the most foundational points
of focus for kingdom living. As kingdom people we are
called to be a "kingdom of priests," fulfilling the mission
ancient Israel never realized. How?

First, by glorifying the Lord through our sacrifices of worship, welcoming His presence with power into our present
world scene. Second, by our obedient lives of purity before
Him, demonstrating the joy and liberty God's way affords.
And third, as the priests ministered healing under the Old
Testament covenant, we minister Christ's wholeness to our
world today. Worshipping priests of the New Testament
are mighty instruments of kingdom expansion.

Kingdom of God

Kingdom Power—Part 1

Your throne is established from of old; You are from everlasting.
Psalm 93:2

When Jesus first commissioned His disciples, He said, "You shall receive power after the Holy Spirit has come upon you" (Acts 1:8). As emissaries of His kingdom (that is, His rule intended to release from sin and to evict all evil powers) we have been commissioned to receive the same power by the same Spirit. To *move* freely in the power of the Holy Spirit, we first need to be *filled,* then we need to remain *focused.* This "fullness" comes at the feet of Jesus, while clear "focus" is sustained at the foot of the Father's Throne.

Psalm 93 brings us to God's Throne with an announcement of His universe-wide reign, declaring the mightiness of "the Lord on high" (v. 4). How like Isaiah's words: "I saw the Lord, high and lifted up" (Is. 6:1) are those of the Lord's Prayer: "For Yours is the kingdom and the power and the glory forever. Amen!" (Matt. 6:13). Such passages as these join to today's text to call us before God's throne with appropriate worship, humility and dependency. It is from this posture of praise that true "kingdom power" generates and endures, for our *focus* is kept on *Him* as the fountain head of kingdom power.

Kingdom of God

Kingdom Power—Part 2

And with great power the apostles gave witness . . . and great grace was upon them all.   *Acts 4:33*

Spirit-filled living is power-filled living. Kingdom power is that enablement given us through the anointing of the Holy Spirit who has been given to transmit the King's love and grace, works and wonders, through us as His servants and ministers—all of us!

But there is a common vulnerability we all share. Like Simon of Samaria, we may fall prey to a human hunger for power for its own sake, instead of understanding that God's power has been given to us for the sake of others. (See Simon's error in Acts 8:14–25.)

To block the entrance of such erroneous misunderstanding, two rules are to be remembered:

First, power for today requires fresh fullness for today. Ephesians 5:18, 19 points the way: *"Keep on being filled* with the Spirit."

Second, God's power is always attended by His grace. As our text shows, a *graciousness* will be present in the manner kingdom power is ministered. Further, because it is God's doing—by grace, not human works—only He will be glorified. Here are kingdom people at their best!

Kingdom of God

Kingdom Duty

Therefore the kingdom of heaven is like a certain king who wanted to settle accounts with his servants.   Matthew 18:23

These words are among the most important any of us will study as potential candidates for kingdom living and for the exercise of kingdom power. They open one of the most penetrating parables Jesus ever taught, for the truth it contains crowds to the center of our souls and forces us to confront an inescapable priority: *forgiveness.*

Jesus relates all responsible citizenship in His kingdom to our readiness and willingness to relay to others the same spirit of forgiveness God has shown us. As He has taught us to pray, "Forgive us our debts as we forgive our debtors" (Matt. 6:12), so this parable elaborates the point. It is shockingly clear. This passage (Matt. 18:23–35) essentially says, "I'm holding you accountable to forgive just as completely as you have been forgiven." And then the message punches home even more forcibly, bringing this conclusion. If we don't settle our accounts by *being* forgiving, God is going to settle a rough account with us!

How much more blessed—how simple and joyous—to simply forgive. How can I do otherwise? He's shown such mercy to me!

Kingdom of God

Kingdom Trials

I John, both your brother and companion in the tribulation and kingdom and patience of Jesus Christ . . .   *Revelation 1:9*

John opens the majestic revelation he received on the Isle of Patmos with a splendidly balanced greeting. Kingdom life is given breadth and perspective here by this most durable of the disciples, who lived for Christ more than sixty years after the Lord ascended to glory. Now, exiled to an island maximum security prison as an enemy of the state, John had "seen it all."

This man spanned the whole panorama of ministry with miracles and signs of God's gracious kingdom power. He's the one who reminds us of Jesus' words: "The works that I do shall you who follow me do—*and greater than these!*" (John 14:12). He is no doubter of miracle might.

Yet here we see the apostle imprisoned and in a place of apparent helplessness. It's a healthy reminder of two things: (1) Kingdom people do not always gain immediate victories; but, (2) Jesus always comes to be with His kingdom's people in the midst of their trials! (Look at verses 10–20, which contain the most magnificent picture of Christ in the entire Bible.) It is encouraging to hear John place the words "tribulation" (i.e., trials and troubles) in the same phrase as "kingdom" (authority and victory). Kingdom people aren't immune to hard times, but, praise God, the King always meets them there!

Kingdom of God

Kingdom Triumph

And He has on his robe and on His thigh a name written: KING OF KINGS AND LORD OF LORDS. Revelation 19:16

he message of the kingdom of God (1) *throbs* in the teaching of our Lord Jesus during His earthly ministry, (2) was *taught* to His disciples as "the Gospel of the Kingdom" they were to preach, and (3) provided the *thrust* of the early Church's witness. So today, we hold this timeless message—proclaiming "The King *has come* and His kingdom is present today with power!" And at the same time we declare, "The King is *coming* and His kingdom will someday be manifest in even greater glory!" The Revelation shows us how this dual vision converges as one message.

In Revelation 12 we see *the Church warring*. There are casualties and there are victories; there are struggles and there are moments of mighty overcoming. The testimony of the Lamb, overcoming through the Blood and proclaimed through the Word, is ours to hold forth as He is manifesting kingdom power now! But the ultimate display of kingdom power awaits the final day. As Jesus Himself leads the final charge against all forms of evil, we see *the Church winning* (Rev. 14). Until then we serve Him in the confidence of "kingdom triumphs"—now and evermore!

Kingdom of God

The Work of Christ

The One Sacrifice

With His own blood He entered the Most Holy Place once for all, having obtained eternal redemption.   Hebrews 9:12

This epistle contrasts God's covenants through Moses and Christ. The Mosaic covenant provided animal sacrifices that brought only temporary relief to man's guilt and demonstrated the lessons of God's justice. But 1 Corinthians 10:6 tells us that the Old Testament sacrifices were given to us as examples, and these sacrifices were symbolic of the perfect sacrifice, the Lamb of God (John 1:29).

Under the old covenant, the High Priest, after purifying himself and offering a sacrifice for his own sin, entered the Holy of Holies to offer a sacrifice for the sins of the nation. These sacrifices had to be repeated annually at the tabernacle, but Jesus, our High Priest, made one sacrifice with His own blood to obtain for us eternal salvation.

Because of Christ's one perfect sacrifice, all believers have access to the Mercy Seat, the very throne of God. We are now invited to "come boldly to the throne of grace, that we may obtain mercy and find grace to help in time of need" (Heb. 4:16). Let us go there today!

Work of Christ

Healing—Part 1

I am the Lord who heals you.   *Exodus 15:26*

One of the most basic truths of Scripture is that God reaches to us, offering His life to transform all aspects of our lives. Salvation is God's rescue of the entire person, and healing is His complete repair of that person. This text emphasizes God's healing work. The Hebrew word *rapha'* means "to cure, repair, mend, restore to health." The main reference of *rapha'* is to physical healing, though it may also be used in relation to the healing of a soul (Ps. 41:4) and the healing of a broken heart (Ps. 147:3).

Some have attempted to limit God's healing power to the spirit or soul, but Exodus 15:26 speaks of physical maladies and their divine cure. The first mention of *rapha'* in the Bible (Gen. 20:17) refers unquestionably to the cure of a physical condition, as in healing from leprosy and boils (Lev. 13:18; 14:3).

Therefore, Scripture affirms and we believe and receive it: "I am the Lord your Physician."

Healing—Part 2

If you diligently heed the voice of the Lord your God . . . I will
put none of the diseases on you. Exodus 15:26

The Lord is a covenant-making and covenant-keeping God. He does not deal with us on the basis of random promises, but takes the initiative of entering into a covenant with His people. A modern synonym of "covenant" is "contract." People like to do business on the basis of a contract, where all the contingencies for both sides are spelled out.

God has clearly spelled out what He will do for us. He has promised to keep His people free from diseases, but He conditions the promise upon our diligent obedience. This is not only a spiritual concept, but also an intensely physical one.

The covenant is made absolutely certain by the fact that God joins His mighty name to the promise, calling Himself *Yahweh-Rapha,* meaning "the Lord who heals." This is one of the compound names by which God revealed His attributes to Israel. Here His very name declares it is His nature to be the Healer to those who obey His word. Remember that our Lord will always act according to His nature. Ask Him now!

Work of Christ

Progressive Healing

And so it was that as they went, they were cleansed.   Luke 17:14

Divine healing does not always happen in an instant. The nature of some healing as progressive is noted in the words, "as they went, they were cleansed."

Not all healing is at the moment of prayer. Instant healings are often expected, but this illustrates the healing in process over a period of time following prayer, and in obedience to Jesus' command, "Go . . . to the priests." As they went in obedience, they were healed. When healing is not instantaneous, we ought not to doubt, but find a possible path of obedience.

In another case of delayed healing (Mark 8:22–25), Jesus anoints and prays for a blind man twice before his healing is perfect. No explanation is given for the delay. However, we could draw from the example that if healing does not happen at once, keep asking, praying for faith, and drawing closer to the Lord.

In the midst of whatever physical affliction we may face, we must learn from these examples by kneeling in prayer, standing in faith, and walking in obedience.

Work of Christ

The Lord's Supper

The cup of blessing which we bless, is it not the communion of the blood of Christ? The bread which we break, is it not the communion of the body of Christ? 1 Corinthians 10:16

The Passover celebration was to be the last meal that Christ would share with the disciples before His death (John 16:28). It was also the setting in which He chose to bring New Covenant thought to an Old Covenant act. Now receiving the bread and the cup is a participation in the body and blood of Christ. While we do not believe that the bread and cup become Christ's actual physical body, we do believe that in partaking by faith we receive the pardon these elements symbolize.

The mystery involved in the covenant meal extends beyond our relationship with Christ and to our relationship with one another. Partakers of the covenant meal also participate in the celebration of the unity of the body in Christ because the breaking of bread points to the fact that each of us is a part of the whole which was broken for us (1 Cor. 10:17).

Let us reach upward to the Father and outward to one another as we partake of the "communion of the body of Christ."

Work of Christ

Gifts of Healing

. . . to another gifts of healings by the same Spirit.

1 Corinthians 12:9

Physical restoration was of such importance that a special spiritual gift of healing was bestowed upon the church. Many examples of the exercise of this gift are found in the book of Acts (3:1–8; 8:5–7; 14:8, 9; 19:11, 12; 28:7, 8).

Healing is mentioned three times in 1 Corinthians 12, and each time it is referred to in the plural: "gifts of healings." The clear intent is that the supernatural healing of the sick should be a permanent ministry established in the church, alongside and abetting the work of evangelizing the world (vv. 4–11, 28). This is for today—timeless—for "the gifts and the calling of God are irrevocable" (Rom. 11:29).

Through the Holy Spirit, God gives all gifts in the name of Jesus. If you need healing today, ask in prayer believing, request the prayer of other believers, and call for the elders of the church to pray. Do not wait to pray until a serious problem arises; begin today to take all needs immediately to the Lord!

Justification

. . . being justified freely by His grace through the redemption that is in Christ Jesus, whom God set forth as a propitiation by His blood, through faith. Romans 3:24, 25

The word "propitiation" is a difficult term, meaning "to appease wrath." Man in his sin cannot approach a God of justice who must judge sin. God's justice can be appeased only by the punishment of sin. But God in His love desires fellowship with man whom He created in His image.

Fellowship with a holy God could only be realized through atoning for the sins that separated mankind from God and His covenant promises. So God presented Jesus as the sacrifice for atonement or reconciliation with separated mankind. It is the shed blood of Christ that ultimately satisfied the requirements of God's justice. God's judgment was fully put upon Christ, the blameless sacrifice, for all sin both past and present. And it is only through faith in the blood of Christ that mankind is justified in God's eyes.

The blood of Christ then becomes the bond that joins people to God, entitling them to God's covenant provisions and providing right relationship with Him. The blood of Christ guarantees our standing as children of the holy God!

Work of Christ

Abiding in Health

No evil shall befall you, nor shall any plague come near your dwelling.   *Psalm 91:10*

This passage promises protection from sickness as a blessing of the redeemed life. Here the Lord describes an abiding defense against "inflicted" disease, but the promise is conditioned upon making the Lord our true refuge and habitation.

When we make the Lord our refuge and habitation by trusting Him—taking our cares, fears, and needs to Him; by seeking His counsel, spending times of refreshing with Him; and by loving Him and walking closely with Him through every day—we enter into a sheltered place of promise regarding health. This truth safeguards against making prayer for healing only a recourse for emergencies. It encourages us to constantly abide with Him and to confirm the wonderful promise of the Lord Jesus, "If you abide in Me, and My words abide in you, you will ask what you desire, and it shall be done for you" (John 15:7).

Where are you living today? Come and make the Lord your habitation . . . there is no better abiding place!

Full Atonement

*He was wounded for our transgressions . . . and by His stripes
we are healed.*
                                                    Isaiah 53:5

Seven hundred years before Christ's birth Isaiah prophesied that the coming Savior would suffer and die for our redemption. He was wounded and bruised for our sins, and He was beaten with stripes for our bodily healing.

The Hebrew words for "griefs" and "sorrows" (v. 4) specifically mean physical affliction. This is verified in the fact that Matthew 8:17 quotes this text as, "He Himself took our infirmities and bore our sicknesses." Further, that the words "borne" and "carried" (v. 4) refer to Jesus' atoning work on the cross is made clear by the fact that they are the same words used to describe Christ's bearing our sins (Is. 53:11; 1 Pet. 2:24). These texts link our salvation and our healing to the atoning work of Calvary. The healing stream that flows from the cross restores both soul and body.

Neither is automatically appropriated, however, for each provision—a soul's eternal salvation or a person's physical healing—must be received by faith. Christ's work on the cross makes this possible. Come in faith today.

Work of Christ

Confession—Part 1

So Miriam was shut out of the camp seven days, and the people did not journey on till Miriam was brought in again.

Numbers 12:15

When Miriam, the sister of Moses, sinned through spiritual pride, she was afflicted with leprosy. Through Moses' intercessory prayer she was healed. Before she experienced healing and restoration, however, she was shut out of the fellowship of the camp until seven days of repentance passed. Not only was Miriam's fellowship interrupted, the whole camp delayed its march until Miriam was restored.

"Confess your trespasses to one another . . . that you may be healed," commands James (James 5:16). Is it possible that delays in receiving answers to our prayer may sometimes be the result of a sin? Is there anything of sin in our hearts that is halting our progress in the Lord, as well as the progress of those around us?

By no means is bodily affliction *always* the result of sin. Nonetheless, when we seek healing, it is wise to search our hearts. Repentance and humility will not earn healing, but they may, as with Miriam, clear the way for God's grace to be revealed more fully.

Confession—Part 2

The blood of Jesus Christ His Son cleanses us from all sin.

1 John 1:7

God is a God of light. Those who are His children do not walk in darkness. Though we have passed from darkness to light, we have not reached perfection. While we have become "new creatures," we have not yet fully escaped our sin nature. While we no longer walk in darkness, John states that we deceive ourselves if we say that we have no sin.

In spite of our sin, we do not have to face judgment alone! Jesus Christ is our Advocate (our defender or attorney) before the eternal justice of the Father (1 John 2:1). Sin's price must be paid. Jesus can free us from the guilt of sin because He has already suffered the penalty for sin on the cross.

Thus, we have the remedy for sin: "If we confess our sins, He is faithful and just to forgive us" (1 John 1:9). Let us bring any unconfessed sin to the Lord today. Then let us live in the light.

Work of Christ

Power of the Blood

And they overcame him by the blood of the Lamb.

Revelation 12:11

Christian believers are involved in a conflict. In this chapter, our enemy is called "the serpent," "the Devil," "Satan," and "the accuser of our brethren" (v. 9, 10). He began this conflict in the Garden of Eden and will continue until the Lord returns to reign.

The good news is that Satan, our enemy, is a defeated foe! Christ's atoning death and resurrection accomplished his complete and final defeat. The blood of Christ the Lamb causes God's people to prevail because it answers all of the enemy's accusations. Satan controls and defeats humankind through guilt and accusations. He is a black-mailer. However, the saints know that the blood has satisfied all of the charges against them, joined them to God, and provided them with every necessary provision to defeat Satan!

God has declared us righteous and victorious, and in the Apostle John's revelation of the final conflict, the message came through: "They overcame [Satan] by the blood of the Lamb." *Our* power to overcome is the same!

Repentance and Healing

And the Lord restored Job's losses when he prayed for his friends.
Job 42:10

Some point to Job as proof that sickness is God's will for many people. While it is true that God permitted Job's illness to show Satan that Job would not turn from his Lord in the face of adversity, it is important to see that the affliction was a direct work of the devil (2:2). When God later healed him and restored his losses, the Hebrew text literally refers to his recovery as a return from captivity, an evidence that his restoration was a driving back of evil, a recovering of something that had been "captured from him" (42:10).

Job's healing also coincides with repentance. Chapter 29 seems to reveal that Job was extremely self-centered, and he repented later (42:5, 6). Job's changed attitude and God's restoration are linked. And Job's spirit of forgiveness toward his friends became pivotal for his own well-being and for theirs (42:7–9).

As we seek the Lord for healing, let us also ask Him to reveal any areas in our lives that require repentance and forgiveness.

Work of Christ

Atonement

For Adam and his wife the Lord God made tunics of skin, and clothed them.   *Genesis 3:21*

When Adam and Eve disobeyed God, they were overcome with guilt. They hid themselves in a remote corner of the garden and tried to cover themselves with fig leaves. Leaves hid their shame, but their sin required a sacrificial covering. The sacrifice of innocent animals to provide garments of skin as a covering for Adam and Eve foreshadows the substitutionary atonement of Christ. It points toward judgment upon the innocent for the sake of the guilty.

Under the new covenant, we are required to be clothed with Christ rather than with our own good works (Eph. 2:8, 9). Christ, by His substitutionary atoning death on the cross, provides the covering we need. The sacrificial animals were only a type of the infinite Lamb of God, Creator of everything, whose death atoned for everyone who would believe.

Whenever there is sin or shame in our lives, it can be dealt with only in Christ Jesus. He alone can bring forgiveness and release from condemnation. And He will. For each one of us. Come to Him today.

Work of Christ

Touch the Lord

Now a woman . . . came from behind and touched the border of
His garment.   Luke 8:43, 44

Here simple, positive faith draws upon the matchless mercy of Jesus. At once Jesus responds to the sick woman's faith with the question, "Who touched Me?" The disciples wondered at the question because Jesus was being thronged by crowding multitudes. Yet, Jesus' question demonstrated that there is a difference between merely thronging Him and touching Him with faith to receive.

The woman's touch was one of desperation. Years of trying remedy after remedy had failed. Her disease made her ceremonially unclean, unable to participate in worship; she was violating Mosaic law by even being in a crowd.

Her touch was also a touch of faith. She said, "If only I may touch His garment, I shall be made well" (Matt. 9:21). We should not wait until we are desperate to go to Jesus; He has promised to answer faith.

Finally, her touch was a touch of becoming. Jesus said, "Somebody touched Me," and went on to call her "Daughter." When you come to Jesus you become somebody: you become a child of God (1 John 3:1, 2).

Work of Christ

Forgiveness and Healing

Forget not all His benefits: who forgives all your iniquities, who heals all your diseases. Psalm 103:2, 3

This is an Old Testament promise of bodily healing based upon the character of Yahweh as the Healer. It is clear that the dimension of healing promised here is specifically to include physical wholeness. The text reinforces the healing covenant, since the Hebrew word translated "diseases" is from the same root as the word for "disease" in Exodus 15:26.

Further, the words for "heal" are the same in both passages, the distinct meaning involving the idea of mending or curing. The two texts form a strong bond and bear witness from the Old Testament that the Lord not only forgives iniquities, but heals our diseases.

If under the former covenant bodily healing was pointedly included with the Father's many other benefits, we can rejoice and rest in faith. The new covenant "glory" exceeds everything of the old (2 Cor. 3:7–11), and we can be certain that God, in Christ, has made a complete provision for the well-being of our total person.

Our Passover Lamb

By faith he kept the Passover and the sprinkling of blood, lest he who destroyed the firstborn should touch them.   Hebrews 11:28

Hebrews 11 is often referred to as the "Faith Hall of Fame" because it goes through Scripture naming great men and women of faith. We read that by faith and in obedience to God's command Moses kept the Passover, the Jewish nation's principle feast celebrated annually.

The death angel's visit was the last of a series of plagues against Pharaoh, who refused to free the children of Israel from Egyptian bondage. To protect the firstborn of every Israelite home, the blood of a lamb was to be put upon the door posts, declaring that the innocent lamb had died in place of the firstborn (Ex 12:1–14). Because the death angel passed over those homes, the lamb became known as the Passover lamb.

Jesus, at His death, fulfilled the symbolism of the Passover (Luke 22:19, 20; 1 Cor. 5:7). He became our Passover lamb, and has now "delivered us from the power of darkness and conveyed us into the kingdom of the Son of His love" (Col. 1:13).

Work of Christ

Healing and Forgiveness

[Jesus answered,] "Which is easier, to say, 'Your sins are forgiven you,' or to say, 'Rise up and walk'?"   *Luke 5:23*

While not all affliction is the result of a specific sin, in this case sin was the cause, for Jesus' first words were, "Your sins are forgiven you." In many cases prayer for healing should begin with confession of sin and repentance (James 5:16; 1 John 1:8, 9).

Jesus' linking of healing with forgiveness is also evidence that human wholeness at every point of need is His concern. Obviously, forgiveness of sins is our greater need, but Jesus affirmed His concern for every part of our being when He taught, "The Spirit of the Lord . . . has anointed Me to preach the gospel to the poor (salvation) . . . to heal the brokenhearted (emotional wholeness) . . . to proclaim liberty to the captives (freedom) and recovery of sight to the blind (healing)" (Luke 4:18).

Jesus is fully able to meet your need—spirit, soul, and body. Where is His touch needed in your life today?

Work of Christ

Steps of Obedience

So he went down and dipped seven times in the Jordan, according to the saying of the man of God; and his flesh was restored.

2 Kings 5:14

Naaman would not have known anything about God's healing power had it not been for an Israelite girl serving in his household. One day she told his wife of Jehovah God's willingness to heal his leprosy. He went to visit the prophet Elisha, and health was given to him as he took the steps of obedience the prophet prescribed. And thus, a pagan general became a worshiper of Jehovah (2 Kings 5:17–19).

Believers do well when they recognize both the saving and healing power of Jesus. God knows how to deal with each person. Naaman was instructed to dip seven times in the Jordan River, and this displeased him. His human brashness and hidden pride surfaced, but his obedience and submission opened the way to health.

The commands of the Lord are so simple and attainable! As He instructed the Israelites in the wilderness to "look and live" (Num. 21:8) to receive their healing, so here the command is simply "wash and be clean."

Work of Christ

The Way to Life

It shall be that everyone who is bitten, when he looks at it, shall live.   *Numbers 21:8*

The plague of fiery serpents sent upon God's people was, in reality, a self-inflicted punishment, resulting from their frequent murmuring. God's judgment was in allowing what their own presumption invited. But in answer to His people's repentance, God prescribed the erecting of a bronze serpent to which all might look in faith and be healed.

The same hope is present today. Jesus said, "As Moses lifted up the serpent in the wilderness, even so must the Son of Man be lifted up, that whoever believes in Him should not perish but have eternal life" (John 3:14). He clearly says that the bronze serpent typified His being raised upon the cross. Our healing, both spiritual and physical, comes from looking to and identifying with Christ crucified, "by whose stripes you were healed" (1 Pet. 2:24).

Jesus, in dying on the cross, offered us a way to life; all we need to do is look and live. Whatever you need today, whether it is freedom for the soul or health for the body, the promise is there for you.

Work of Christ

Healing Through Prayer

*Paul went in to him and prayed, and he laid his hands on him
and healed him.*

Acts 28:8

Here is a reference to divine healings, in spite of the
fact that Luke, a physician, accompanied Paul. This
fact is so troublesome to critics of modern miraculous healings that some have come forth with the theory that the
healings mentioned in verse 9 were the work of Luke who
used medical remedies, although Luke is not mentioned by
name.

The theory is based on the use of the Greek word for
"healed" (v. 8), which some insist refers to medical therapy
alone. This word, however, is used thirty-two times in
Scripture with reference to divine healing.

This observation is not to say that medical treatment is
wrong. It is not. However, it does clarify that this text is not
grounds for the substitution of medical therapy for prayer.
God heals by many means: the prayer of faith, natural
recuperative power, medical aid or medicine, miracles—all
are gifts from His hand (James 1:17).

Work of Christ

Redemption

You were not redeemed with corruptible things, like silver or gold . . . but with the precious blood of Christ.   *1 Peter 1:18, 19*

Another name for Christian believers is "the redeemed" (Is. 62:12). To redeem means to buy back, to buy out of debt or out of bondage, to set free by the payment of a price.

The redeemer pays a worthy price to reclaim something previously owned. Mankind was once God's by creation, but became lost through sin. God offers Christ's blood to us as our substitutionary sacrifice and accepts it when we offer it back to Him. Our transaction with God is therefore not a gold-and-silver economy; it is a life-and-death economy. Christ gave His life's blood to buy us out of sin and death. His blood is a worthy price and provides an imperishable bond between us and God.

Therefore we can rejoice in the fact that Jesus "gave Himself for us, that He might redeem us from every lawless deed and purify for Himself His own special people, zealous for good works" (Titus 2:14). Let us praise Him today; we are the redeemed!

An Only Son

So Abraham went and took the ram, and offered it up for a burnt offering instead of his son.   Genesis 22:13

Abraham was commanded by God to offer as a sacrifice his only son, Isaac. Being a man of faith, Abraham set out to obey God, in spite of the fact that it contradicted God's previous promise that Abraham's seed would bless the whole world (Gen. 17:1–3). Abraham believed that God would keep his covenant (Heb. 11:17–19), and God did provide another sacrifice: a ram caught in a bush.

This dramatically foreshadows God's offering His only begotten Son to die in our place (John 3:16). God's covenant love gave Abraham a son, and covenant love provided a substitutionary sacrifice to save that son. Centuries later covenant love would cause God to give His own Son as a blood sacrifice for the sons of men.

Now He says to each of us, "He who did not spare His own Son, but delivered Him up for us all, how shall He not with Him also freely give us all things?" (Rom. 8:32). Let us live in the fullness of that promise today.

Work of Christ

Redeemed by the Blood

It is the blood that makes atonement for the soul. Leviticus 17:11

Believers in Christ have often been criticized for their emphasis upon the blood of Jesus. However, "blood" occurs 360 times in the Old Testament and more than fifty times in the New Testament with reference to atonement. Moses declares in Leviticus that life is in the blood and that only blood can make atonement for sin.

From the first sacrifice, when God killed animals to make coverings for Adam and Eve, a sacrifice has been required to atone for sin. The truth conveyed is that an innocent one substitutes for the guilty. Romans 6:23 declares that "the wages of sin is death." We deserve death for our sinful deeds, but Jesus gave His life that we might live, and now offers that life to all who will believe in Him.

Let us never be ashamed of the gospel of salvation through the blood of Jesus. Rather, let us join the heavenly throng in singing, "Redeemed by the blood of the Lamb!"

Work of Christ

Proclaim Healing

Heal the sick there, and say to them, "The kingdom of God has come near to you."
Luke 10:9

*I*n this text, Jesus sends out seventy of His followers to preach the gospel of the kingdom and to heal the sick. The coming of God's kingdom and the ministry of healing are not separated. Earlier, Jesus had sent out the twelve disciples with the same message (Luke 9:1, 2). It becomes clear that Jesus' intent is for the ministry of healing to be part of the declaration of the coming of His kingdom.

Jesus devoted a large part of His ministry to healing the sick. This ministry of healing was experienced throughout the book of Acts, and in James 5:13–16 is declared as one of the responsibilities of eldership in a local congregation. The sick are healed today, demonstrating the continued presence of the kingdom of God.

The Holy Spirit delights to confirm the kingdom's presence by glorifying the King's power and verifying Jesus Christ's work through the ministry of healing. Come to Him today for your healing; He is waiting to receive you now!

Work of Christ

Justification

Having now been justified by His blood, we shall be saved from wrath through Him.

Romans 5:9

"There is none righteous, no, not one," declares Romans 3:10, establishing that all people are unrighteous and therefore deserving of judgment. But God's covenant love reaches beyond the fulfillment of justice to establish a bond of fellowship in the blood of Jesus Christ. Because of Christ's atoning work we now stand before the Father as righteous! This is the essence of "justification."

Justification is mentioned throughout the New Testament. Paul says that we are justified by faith (Rom. 5:1); we must believe in Christ, and by grace (Rom. 3:24) our salvation is a free gift. James contends for justification by works (James 2:21)—our lives must demonstrate the change that God has worked in our souls.

Just once in the New Testament are we said to be justified by the "blood." This means that Christ took our sin and guilt on the cross, erasing all condemnation against us. Faith in His blood not only brings our deliverance from the wrath of God, but also is the means of victorious living through participation in His life.

The Covenant-Maker

God called the light Day, and the darkness He called Night.
Genesis 1:5

God is revealed, from the beginning, as a covenant-making and covenant-keeping God. Jeremiah referred to God's activity at creation as acts of covenant (Jer. 33:20), speaking of God's "covenant with the day" and "covenant with the night." Through this, God's unchangeable character is shown to us each day as surely as the sun rises and sets. Jeremiah then goes on to say that God could no more break His covenant of redemption with His people than He could violate His covenant with nature (v. 21).

God has also made a covenant with all who will believe in, confess, and accept His Son, the Lord Jesus Christ. This covenant was sealed with the blood of Calvary's cross. All that God has promised to do for us, He will fulfill.

Jeremiah later wrote that the Lord's mercies are new every day, and His faithfulness is great to us (Lam. 3:22, 23). Praise the Lord today that He keeps His covenant. Just as we are sure that the sun will rise, we are equally as sure of His faithfulness toward us!

Work of Christ

An Atmosphere of Faith

If you can believe, all things are possible to him who believes.
Mark 9:23

In this passage Jesus tells us that "believing" is the condition for answered prayer for a healing. The father of the demon-possessed boy answered in tears, "I believe," then added, "Help my unbelief!" Since faith is a gift, we may pray for it as this father did. Note how quickly God's grace answered!

Jesus rebuked the disciples because they could not cast out the mute spirit, calling them "faithless" (v. 19). In Matthew's account of this incident, Jesus said that if one has faith as a mustard seed he can move a mountain (Matt. 17:20).

But there is another lesson to be learned: where an atmosphere of unbelief makes it difficult to believe, we should seek a different setting. Even Jesus' ability to work miracles was reduced where unbelief prevailed (Matt. 13:58). As we go through the day, let us not diminish Jesus' ability to work in us. Prayer and praise provide an atmosphere of faith in God and welcome His presence in our lives.

Work of Christ

Attitude of Heart

I do not delight in the blood of bulls.   Isaiah 1:11

The Bible declares that without the shedding of blood there is no remission of sin (Heb. 9:22). Jesus confirmed this truth with His death on the cross. How, then, do we understand God's admonition to Isaiah?

Even the most sacred acts become meaningless when we thoughtlessly perform them while living in open disobedience to God's will. In Isaiah's day, the sacrifices and feasts had come to be only outward forms, devoid of true devotion and righteous living. The ultimate issue in sacrifice is the attitude of the heart. Right relationship, not mere ceremony, is the goal of God's covenant-making activity.

Nothing will ever diminish the completeness of Christ's atoning sacrifice, but we can grieve the Holy Spirit by meaningless conformity to form without genuine worship and enlightened service.

Today, let us make sure our heart-attitude is right before the Father as we cry out with the psalmist, "You do not desire sacrifice . . . [but] the sacrifices of God are a broken spirit, a broken and contrite heart" (Ps. 51:16, 17).

Work of Christ

Our Peacemaker

. . . to reconcile all things to Himself, . . . having made peace through the blood of His cross.   *Colossians 1:20*

Christ Jesus is the matchless peacemaker. Through His death, He reconciled to the Father all of creation, especially a humanity alienated from God by sin. Jesus was able to accomplish this reconciliation because "in Him all the fullness" dwelled (v. 19). He was fully God and fully human. He could die for mankind because as a man He had no sins of His own; He could die for all of creation because as the Creator He had a higher value than creation. Thereby He was able to provide the means for all of creation to be reconciled to God.

Because sin takes life, life is required to repay sin's debts. Jesus Christ gave His life in blood to satisfy all of mankind's sin debts and to restore covenant peace between God and man. "For [Jesus] Himself is our peace, who has made both one, and has broken down the middle wall of separation" (Eph. 2:14). Let us live in that peace, with the Prince of Peace as our sovereign (Is. 9:6) and His rule of love as our law (James 2:8).

Increasing Faith

Seed and Harvest

While the earth remains, seedtime and harvest, cold and heat, winter and summer, and day and night shall not cease.

Genesis 8:22

The first thing Noah did after the Flood was to build an altar and make a sacrifice to the Lord. God was pleased with Noah and made promises to the human family through the faith of Noah. One of the promises given at this time was the Law of Seedtime and Harvest: "While the earth remains, seedtime and harvest . . . shall not cease."

When God created the first living thing, He gave it the ability to grow and multiply. How? Through the principle of seed and harvest. Your life began by this principle, and since your birth your life has operated by this same principle. Harvest springs from the good or bad seeds you have sown, whether or not you were consciously aware of your seed-planting.

The principle continues today. To overcome life's problems, reach your potential in life, see your life become fruitful, multiplied, replenished (that is, in health, finance, spiritual renewal, family—your entire being), determine to follow God's law of seedtime and harvest.

Sow the seed of His promise in the soil of your need!

Increasing Faith

A New Name

No longer shall your name be called Abram, but your name shall be Abraham; for I have made you a father of many nations.

Genesis 17:5

The Bible throughout its pages teaches us the importance of the words we speak. In this text God changes Abram's name to Abraham and promises Abraham that he will become the father of many nations. "Abram" means "High Father" or "Patriarch." "Abraham" means "Father of a Multitude." Thus, God was arranging that every time Abraham heard or spoke his own name, he would be reminded of God's promise.

By the change of his name, God was promising to Abraham that the focus of his life was not to be on himself or on his position, not even on what God would make him to be. No, now the goal of Abraham's life was to be others, how God would use him to touch countless others with the life and blessing of God.

The principle is clear: Let God's words, which designate His will and promise for your life, become as fixed in your mind and as governing of your speech as God's changing the name of Abraham was in shaping his concept of himself.

Do not "name" yourself anything less than God does!

Increasing Faith

Patience and Faith

Let us go up at once and take possession, for we are well able to overcome it.   Numbers 13:30

Caleb saw the same giants and walled cities as the other spies, but the ten spies brought back a "bad report" of unbelief. Caleb, however, declared a conviction, a confession, before all Israel: "We are well able to overcome it." He along with the others had carefully surveyed the land; he had seen, so his faith was not blind. Faith does not deny the reality of the difficulty; rather, it declares the power of God in the face of the problem.

Though his faith-filled report was rejected by the majority, Caleb stood his ground in faith, but still moved in partnership and support alongside those whose unbelief delayed his own experience. He demonstrated a remarkable combination of faith and patience. Caleb's eventual possession of the land at a later date indicates that even though delays come, the declaration of faith will ultimately bring victory to the believer.

Let patience and faith work together to see you through the struggle and into the fulfillment of the promise.

Speak in Faith

You shall not shout . . . until the day I say to you, "Shout!" Then
you shall shout. Joshua 6:10

Here Joshua commands Israel to maintain total silence as they walk around the city of Jericho. The memory that Israel's forty-year sojourn in the wilderness was a result of the people's murmuring in unbelief was doubtless in Joshua's mind. Also, the spies had returned with a majority report motivated by what man sees without Holy Spirit-given vision. Their lack of belief that they could take the land had sealed their fate in the desert.

With these lessons of history in mind, Joshua's directive to keep silent teaches a precaution. When facing great challenges, do not permit your tongue to speak unbelieving words. Keep demoralizing speech from your lips. Words can bind up or set free, hence the order of silence. Later they would see the salvation of the Lord following their shout of triumph (Josh. 6:20).

We cannot help what we see and hear, but our refusal to speak doubt and fear will keep our hearts more inclined to what God can do, rather than to what we cannot do (Prov. 30:32).

Increasing Faith

Giving

Nor will I offer burnt offerings to the Lord my God with that which costs me nothing.   2 Samuel 24:24

Araunah tried to give King David land, oxen, and other items for sacrifices, but David insisted on paying Araunah, saying that he could not present to God an offering that cost him nothing.

The heart of faith is that unless you experience some sacrifice, you have not truly given. Until your giving costs you something, something that represents a portion of your very life, then it is not a living gift and will not yield a good harvest. Thus, our giving to God should have these three qualities:

First, it should be our *best.* Because God has given His best to us, we want to give our best to Him.

Second, we should give to God *first.* The first thought in our minds after we have received something should be, "How can I give a portion of this harvest to the work of the Lord?"

Third, our giving should be *generous,* flowing freely and abundantly from our heart. Jesus said, "Freely you have received, freely give" (Matt. 10:8).

Increasing Faith

Sow in Faith

The bin of flour was not used up, nor did the jar of oil run dry,
according to the word of the Lord.   *1 Kings 17:16*

This episode (1 Kin. 17:8–16) teaches us to invite God to work by His unlimited power within our limited circumstances and resources. Two important principles are illustrated here:

First, we must give something out of our need. That is the kind of giving that involves our faith. This woman had a need for herself and her family, but she gave to sustain the life of God's prophet Elijah. Then God multiplied her giving back to her.

Second, the widow gave first, before seeking to meet her own needs. Her giving resulted in the miracle supply of God flowing back into her life. For perhaps as long as three years God multiplied her seed sown.

When we give out of our need and to help others first, we place ourselves in the flow of how God has made life to work for us and not against us. We have sown in our faith, and we reap the harvest of the faithfulness of God.

Sow! Give God something to multiply.

Increasing Faith

Expect to Receive

"What shall we do about the hundred talents which I have given to the troops of Israel?" And the man of God answered, "The Lord is able to give you much more than this." 2 Chronicles 25:9

In human economy, the law of supply and demand regulates the price paid for goods and services. In times of oversupply, prices fall; in times of shortage, prices rise. Our economy fluctuates with the times and seasons.

God's economy, however, has no shortages. God's supply always exceeds our need. He does not want His people to lack, but rather, to "have an abundance for every good work" (2 Cor. 9:8). Do we think that if we give something to God, we will have less? No! We can never outgive God. No matter what we give to Him, He will multiply it back to us in an amount greater than we gave.

Our ability to receive, however, is not automatic. Expecting to receive, like freedom to give, is an act of our faith. The farmer learns that both planting the seed and receiving the harvest are acts of faith.

Is there something you need to give? Then let it go in faith. Is there something you need to receive? Then embrace it in faith.

For seedtime and harvest are in God's hands.

Increasing Faith

Speak in Faith

These people draw near to Me with their mouth, and honor Me with their lips, but their heart is far from Me. Matthew 15:8

Jesus here quotes from Isaiah 29:13 in charging the religious leaders of His day with setting aside God's Word by their traditions. Jesus dismisses their worship because their hearts were not aligned with their lips. Living faith—true worship—requires that the mouth and the heart be together in a unity that prevents any tinge of hypocrisy.

Praises and true faith emanate from lips that draw from the depths of the heart. When speaking in faith flows as a living principle, the words are not a ritual recitation of slogans; such recitation is only acting out a human tradition and, as Jesus indicates, is potentially hypocritical.

Just as we are called to genuine praise and worship, not as pretenders or ritual performers, so let our confessing of God's promises be without hypocrisy. Let us speak what God's Holy Spirit has truly birthed in our hearts, thereby causing us to speak faithfully with our lips.

Has God dropped a promise into your heart? Then speak it forth with the courage of convinced faith and watch Him who gave you the word fulfill it.

Increasing Faith

Mountain-Moving Faith

I say to you, if you have faith as a mustard seed, you will say to this mountain, "Move from here to there," and it will move.
Matthew 17:20

When you plant a seed, God changes the nature of that seed so that it becomes a plant, and the power of life surges into that tender, young plant to such a great extent that even a mountain of earth cannot stop it from pushing upward!

Jesus said that our faith in God is like a seed. When we put our faith into action, that is, when we release it to God, it takes on a totally new nature. It takes on the nature of a miracle in the making.

What is the mountain in your life? Loneliness? Loss of a job? Disease? A wounded relationship? Trouble in your home? Something else? Be encouraged! Jesus shows the way to see that mountain removed! God says you can apply your faith to see your daily needs met.

How? You sow the mustard-seed smallness of your faith into an action of love. Then, when your faith is planted and is growing, speak to your mountain and watch God set about its removal.

Increasing Faith

Whatever You Ask

Have faith in God . . . whatever things you ask when you pray,
believe that you receive them, and you will have them.

Mark 11:22, 24

From Jesus' own lips we receive the most direct and practical instruction concerning our exercise of faith. Consider three points:

1) Faith is to be "in God." Faith that speaks is first faith that seeks. The Almighty One is the source and ground of our faith and being. Faith only flows to Him because of the faithfulness that flows from Him.

2) Faith is not a trick performed with our lips, but a spoken confession that springs from the conviction of our hearts. Faith's confession is not a formula for getting things from God, but Jesus does teach here that the faith in our hearts is to be spoken.

3) Jesus' words "whatever things" apply this principle to every aspect of our lives. The only restrictions are that our faith be in God and in alignment with His will and Word, and that we believe and not doubt.

This "speaking to the mountain" is not a vain or superstitious exercise, or indulgence in humanistic mind-science, but instead becomes an applied release of God's creative word of promise.

Increasing Faith

Abundant Life

I have come that they may have life, and that they may have it
more abundantly.   *John 10:10*

God wants to give all of Himself to you, and, along with Himself, all that He represents and has. Inherent in God's total self is true fullness—the real possibility of health for your total being (body, mind, emotions, relationships), of your material needs being met. Above all, His fullness includes eternal life.

Jesus said that He came to give life—not just ordinary existence, but life in fullness and abundance (3 John 2). On the other hand, the Enemy (Satan) comes only to steal, kill, and destroy. The line is clearly drawn. On one side is God with goodness, life, and plenty of all that is necessary for life (see Joel 2:26; 2 Pet. 1:3), and on the other side is the Enemy of our souls, who comes to rob us of God's blessings, to oppress our bodies through disease and accidents, and to destroy everything that we hold dear.

You begin to experience this biblical fullness as you believe it is God's highest desire for you. You increase in His fullness as you line up your highest desires with His desires for you.

Increasing Faith

Abundant Blessing—Part 1

Give, and it will be given to you: good measure, pressed down, shaken together, and running over will be put into your bosom.

Luke 6:38

*J*esus opened up for us a whole new way of giving. He gave Himself totally to and for the needs of people. We no longer need to pay or sacrifice our way into God's mercy, for Jesus Christ has paid our debt before God and His cross is a completed work in our eternal interest.

Our giving, then, is no longer a debt that we owe, but a seed that we sow! The life and power source are in Him. Ours is simply to act on the potential God has placed in us by His power and grace.

Note that when Jesus said, "Give," He also said, "and it will be given to you." Giving and receiving belong together. As we give we put ourselves in a position to reach out and receive a harvest.

A principle of planting and reaping is that the amount of fruit that results from sowing is disproportionate to the measure of the seed put into the ground. Therefore Jesus said that the harvest will be "good measure, pressed down, shaken together, and running over."

Increasing Faith

Abundant Blessing—Part 2

With the same measure that you use, it will be measured back to you.   *Luke 6:38*

Speaking to people familiar with farms and farmers, Jesus can talk to His audience about principles of harvest. He reminds them that the more seed you plant, the more grain you receive back, not just that a pint of seed brings a pint of wheat. A principle of planting and reaping is that the result is disproportionate to the cause. No matter how much you give, you will always receive more in return. Jesus said, "pressed down, and running over."

Another lesson of the harvest is that the product received may differ in form greatly from the seed that is sown. We should, then, remain sensitive at all times to the different ways in which God may deliver our harvest. The harvest may come to us as an idea, an opportunity, an invitation, or a previously unknown or unidentified association.

Watch expectantly for the ways in which God may choose to deliver the harvest to you in His "due season." For you, it may be *today!*

Jesus' Name

Silver and gold I do not have, but what I do have I give you: In the name of Jesus Christ of Nazareth, rise up and walk. Acts 3:6

*I*n this first recorded miracle performed by the disciples in the Book of Acts, we are given a key for use by all believers in exercising faith's authority. When bringing healing to the lame man, Peter employs the full name and title of our Lord: Jesus Christ [Messiah] of Nazareth.

"Jesus" was a common name in first-century Jewish culture and continues to be used in many places today. But the declaration of His full name and title, a noteworthy practice in Acts, seems a good and practical lesson for us (see Acts 2:22; 4:10). In our confession of faith and as a proclamation of power, speak His deity and lordship as the Christ, the Messiah. Use His precious, personal name as Jesus the Savior.

Call upon Him as Lord Jesus, or Jesus Christ, or Jesus of Nazareth, there being no legal or ritual demand intended in this point. But just as we pray in Jesus' name (John 16:24), so we exercise all authority by the privilege of power He has granted us in His name (Matt. 28:18; John 14:13, 14).

Great Grace

And with great power the apostles gave witness to the resurrection of the Lord Jesus. And great grace was upon them all.

Acts 4:33

Most believers know the common definition of the beautiful word "grace" as "the unmerited favor of God." This is wonderfully true and clearly relates to our salvation apart from the works or energy of our flesh (Eph. 2:7–9).

But "grace" as used in this text and texts such as Luke 2:40 and Acts 11:23, also refers to "operations of the power of God." Just as God in mercy saves us by His grace, so also that grace is manifested in great dynamic where the Holy Spirit is at work in power.

Zechariah 4:7 provides an Old Testament illustration of this truth. The prophet instructed Zerubbabel to speak "grace" to the mountain—the hindrance he faced in the trying task of rebuilding God's temple. Speaking "grace" to obstacles we face is an action of faith, drawing on the operation of God's great power. We only speak: the work is entirely His—by His gracious power and for His great glory.

As we speak God's grace in the face of our mountainous impossibilities, we can see "great power" and "great grace" manifest in our behalf today.

Increasing Faith

Spoken Confession

If you confess with your mouth the Lord Jesus and believe in your heart that God has raised Him from the dead, you will be saved.

Romans 10:9

Here is a foundational lesson in the importance and power of speaking out one's faith. This principle is established at the very beginning of our life in Christ. Just as salvation (God's righteous working in our behalf) is appropriated by heart belief and spoken confession, so His continual working in our lives is advanced by the same means.

God allows, encourages, even requires our active participation in all His gracious dealings with us. He does not force us as slaves to move against our will. He does call to us as sons and daughters in His family to accept our role and responsibility.

So having begun our life in Christ in the spirit of *saving* faith, let us grow now in *active* faith—believing in God's mighty power for all our needs, speaking with our lips what our hearts receive and believe of the many promises in His Word.

Let us accept God's promises for all our needs by endowing them with our confessed belief, just as when we were saved.

Increasing Faith

God's Timetable

And let us not grow weary while doing good, for in due season we shall reap if we do not lose heart.   Galatians 6:9

God has a timetable for every seed we plant, but His timetable is not always our timetable. Sometimes the "due season" means a quick return. Sometimes it means a process or a slow return that may take years—even a lifetime.

But we can count on three things. First, God will cause a harvest to come from the seeds we plant. Second, God is never early or late. He is always right on time with our best interests at heart. Third, our harvest will have the same nature as the seeds we have sown: good seeds bring good harvests; bad seeds bring bad harvests.

What are we to do during the growing time of our seeds? Refuse to become discouraged because God has promised an abundant harvest. Determine to keep faith alive and active by allowing the hope planted in our hearts by the Spirit to flourish. Give and keep on giving, because we know this: His harvest is guaranteed.

The Lord's Table

For as often as you eat this bread and drink this cup, you proclaim the Lord's death till He comes.   1 Corinthians 11:26

Just as water baptism outwardly declares an inward experience of salvation through the blood of the Lord Jesus, so each observance of the Lord's Table is a powerful occasion for faith's confession. In this ordinance, the Christian confesses before all heaven not only that he has believed, but also that he has not forgotten. "In remembrance" involves more than just memory; the word suggests an "active calling to mind."

The word "for" in v. 26 introduces the reason for the repetition of the Supper. It is an acted sermon for it proclaims the Lord's death. The outward act of faith, as the bread and cup are taken, is an ongoing confession. Each occasion of partaking is an opportunity to say, proclaim, or confess again: "I herewith lay hold of all the benefits of Christ's full redemption for my life—forgiveness, wholeness, strength, health, sufficiency."

The Lord's Supper is not simply a ritual remembrance, but a powerful proclamation by which we actively call to memory and appropriate today all that Jesus provided and promised through His cross.

Increasing Faith

Jesus Is Lord

At the name of Jesus every knee should bow, . . . every tongue should confess that Jesus Christ is Lord, to the glory of God the Father.   *Philippians 2:10, 11*

*B*ible scholars note that the word "confess" means "to acknowledge openly and joyfully, to celebrate and give praise." Here we are all called to follow God the Father's exaltation of His Son by fully recognizing and joyfully admitting that Jesus Christ is the Lord of our lives and the Lord of our situation.

All humans, angels, and demon spirits will ultimately bow the knee to Jesus, rendering to Him complete and final homage. That confession of every tongue will one day be heard by every ear as the ultimate and complete rule of Jesus is recognized.

But until that day, our confession of Jesus Christ as Lord invites and receives His presence and power over all evil whenever we face it now. As we admit our own helplessness, as we confess our utter dependence, and as we declare His lordship—in faith—His rule enters those settings and circumstances today.

Increasing Faith

Believe and Receive

Whoever says to this mountain, "Be removed and be cast into the sea," and does not doubt in his heart, but believes . . . he will have whatever he says.   Mark 11:23

Here Jesus makes a strong contrast between doubting and believing. The two produce opposite results. When we believe that God exists and that He loves us and wants to meet our needs, then our believing brings trust into our heart.

On the other hand, doubt can be just as real as faith. The reverse of faith, doubt tells us that God does not exist or that He is unloving and uncaring about our needs. Doubt gives rise to fear, which brings torment, not peace. Doubt and fear then cut us off from the flow of life and blessing which God desires to send our way.

In contrast, faith is openness and receptivity toward God and all His benefits. Expectancy opens our life to God and puts us in a position to receive salvation, joy, health, financial supply, or peace of mind—all the things that doubt wants to steal from us.

Believe and receive everything good your heart longs for, and more!

Increasing Faith

Embracing and Promise

Having seen [the promises] afar off [they] were assured of them, embraced them and confessed that they were strangers and pilgrims on the earth.   *Hebrews 11:13*

Hebrews 11 records glorious victories of faith's champions yet here speaks of those who died "not having received the promises." Still, they died in faith just as they had lived in faith.

The key to understanding this admirable group is that when given a promise by God, they became fully persuaded that the promise was true. Thus they embraced (literally "greeted") that promise in their hearts. They also confessed (admitted and acknowledged) that the focus of their lives was beyond anything they could see in this world, that they were strangers and pilgrims here.

Thus, while each of these persons did receive many victories through faith, the text says that they did not receive everything that was promised. But whether or not they received what they asked and hoped for did not change their behavior nor their steadfast trust in God.

For us as well, faith's worship and walk do not depend on answered or unanswered prayers. Our confession of the lordship of Jesus in our lives is to be consistent—a daily celebration, with deep gratitude.

Increasing Faith

Words of Life

*Let the words of my mouth and the meditation of my heart be
acceptable in Your sight, O Lord, my strength and my Redeemer.*
Psalm 19:14

his oft-quoted verse attests to the importance and
desirability of our words and thoughts being consistent with God's Word and will. The text literally says, "Let
what I *speak* and what my heart murmurs to itself be a
delight to You, God." The truth of this text urges us to
always speak the kind of words that confirm what we
believe or think in our hearts about our Heavenly Father,
His love, and His power.

To believe yet contradict our beliefs with careless words
from our mouth is not acceptable in God's sight. Such
words not only become faithless and fruitless to us, but they
can produce doubts in others—both believers and unbelievers. Rather, Acts 5:19, 20 give a command that is as true
for us as it was for the apostles, "An angel of the Lord . . .
said, 'Go, stand in the temple and speak to the people all
the words of this life.'"

As we go about our daily activities today, let us speak the
words of life that delight the Lord.

Increasing Faith

Giving Everything

He and all who were with him were astonished at the catch of fish
which they had taken.   Luke 5:9

Jesus taught about seed-sowing and the importance of planting in good soil (see Mark 4:1–20). Then, as if to illustrate His point, He told this group of discouraged and tired fishermen to launch out in faith for a miracle catch.

These men had just given Jesus the greatest possession that fishermen have—their boat. Here, Jesus stood and preached the gospel. In that moment, they served the greatest need Jesus had. Then Jesus immediately turned and multiplied that gift back to them in the most practical way, meeting the greatest need they had.

As commercial fishermen, they needed fish in order to make a living. As men, they also needed to see God at work in their lives. They needed to know that Jesus was who He claimed to be. They needed to know faith was in operation. Jesus met all of those needs!

When you give everything to the Lord, from the simplest of things to the greatest, the returns are incredible! And He will reveal Himself to you with all of His grace and power!

Increasing Faith

Conditions to Faith—Part 1

Whoever . . . does not doubt in his heart, but believes that those things he says will be done, he will have whatever he says.

Mark 11:23

Many believers want "easy faith": faith that works like a good luck charm whenever and wherever they want it. But the Bible teaches that faith will require something of us, and throughout Scripture, several conditions must be noted.

This text points out that we are not to doubt (Mark 11:22–24). Those who are double-minded will not receive anything (James 1:6–8). Further, Jesus goes on to say, "Whenever you stand praying, and you have anything against anyone, forgive him, that your Father in heaven may also forgive you" (Mark 11:25). The great hindrance to faith that brings miracle release is unforgiveness. Whether or not the attitude is justified by the circumstances, resentment, bitterness, jealousy, and envy are the obstacles to faith's release. The mountain-moving hand of God must begin in our lives by moving the mountain of hard-heartedness out of our own hearts. To see action through faith, there must be forgiveness and love.

Increasing Faith

Conditions to Faith—Part 2

Diligently heed the voice of the Lord your God and do what is right in His sight.   Exodus 15:26

God asks us to heed Him. We are to have a hearing ear so we will hear Him. God has always spoken to His people, and He will speak to you today, but you must cultivate a habit of listening for His voice. He speaks in many ways: through His Word, through His anointed servants, and through direct revelation in the inner man (Eph. 1:17, 18). He is seeking a people who will *listen* for His voice and not try to run and hide from Him (see Gen. 3:8).

God also asks us to "do what is right in His sight." He is seeking people who will not only *hear* His words, but will take them to heart and *act* on them. He calls us to be people who will obey His word and not be hearers only (James 1:22–25).

As we obey Him, His goodness is abundantly promised. It awaits those who "(sow) to the Spirit" (Gal. 6:7–9), hear the voice of the Lord, and do what He tells them to do.

Conditions of Faith—Part 3

"Bring all the tithes into the storehouse . . . and try Me . . ." says the Lord, "If I will not open . . . the windows of heaven . . . pour out for you such blessing . . . and . . . rebuke the devourer for your sakes."   *Malachi 3:10, 11*

In this passage of Scripture, God actually invites people to *try* (prove) Him—to verify His trustworthiness with their giving. He has given us a "fool-proof" test of His faithfulness! But it first requires a step of faith on our part.

He says that by disobeying Him in the tithe, we rob Him of the privilege of pouring out great and overflowing blessings. He calls for renewed giving with these promises. First, there will be "food" or resources for God's work ("in My house").

Second, He says those who give will be placed in a position to receive great, overflowing blessings. Our obedience releases His faithfulness! You will experience the windows of heaven actually opening with blessings you will not be able to receive or contain!

Third, God says that He will "rebuke the devourer" for your sakes. He will cause every blessing that has your name written on it to be directed to you, and Satan himself cannot stop it.

Do not be afraid to try God with your giving; He is God and He will stand the test every time.

Increasing Faith

Overcoming

And they overcame him by the blood of the Lamb and by the word of their testimony.   *Revelation 12:11*

There is no greater biblical declaration of faith's confession than from those facing the cataclysmic travail of the last days. They endure persecutions in the overcoming power of the blood of the Lamb and of the word of their transforming faith in Christ. Their faith is unwavering, the result of an abiding relationship with Jesus Christ. This is the heart of faith's confession, based in God's Word and the blood of the Lamb, whose victory has provided the eternal conquest of Satan.

With Christ's victory over Satan, those who have maintained their confession of faith now share in His victory. With their sins blotted out and their declaration of Jesus' redemptive work in their lives, they silence the attempts of the prince of darkness to intimidate God's children. His accusing voice of condemnation and guilt is swallowed up in the triumph of Calvary.

Declare your abiding faith and continue in Jesus' ultimate victory, overcoming Satan by the power of the Cross and the steadfastness of your confession of faith in Christ's triumph.

Increasing Faith

God's Faithfulness—Part 1

Great is Your faithfulness.   *Lamentations 3:23*

I have often wondered if we as believers would have more faith in the Lord and trust in His willingness to work on our behalf if we truly recognized the greatness of His faithfulness. A look at the literal meaning of the Hebrew word *'emunah* used here gives us insight into the foundation upon which the Lord calls us to stand.

'Emunah literally means "firmness, stability, faithfulness, fidelity, conscientiousness, steadiness, certainty; that which is permanent, enduring, steadfast." *'Emunah* comes from a word meaning "to be firm, sure, established, and steady." "Amen" is derived from this same word and means "It is firmly, truly so!" *'Emunah* is often translated "faithfulness" or "truth," as truth is considered something ultimately certain, stable, and unchangingly fixed.

No matter what may be shaking in your life today, being rooted in His great faithfulness, we shall stand secure in Him.

Increasing Faith

God's Faithfulness—Part 2

Great is Your faithfulness.   *Lamentations 3:23*

The verse previous to the text reads, "Through the Lord's mercies we are not consumed, because His compassions fail not. They are new every morning. . . ." Let us lift our voices today in praise for His faithful, gracious, sustaining hand that strengthens and guides us through every new day; and that includes today!

Great is thy faithfulness, O God my Father,
There is no shadow of turning with thee;
Thou changest not, thy compassions, they fail not;
As thou hast been thou forever wilt be.

Summer and winter, and springtime and harvest,
Sun, moon, and stars in their courses above
Join with all nature in manifold witness
To thy great faithfulness, mercy, and love.

Pardon for sin and a peace that endureth,
Thine own dear presence to cheer and to guide;
Strength for today and bright hope for tomorrow,
Blessings all mine, with ten thousand beside!

Great is thy faithfulness!
Great is thy faithfulness!
Morning by morning new mercies I see;
All I have needed thy hand hath provided;
Great is thy faithfulness, Lord, unto me!

Increasing Faith

Harvest Guaranteed

If you have faith as a mustard seed, you can say to this mulberry tree, "Be pulled up by the roots and be planted in the sea," and it would obey you. — Luke 17:6

The symbolism of the seed is used throughout Scripture. In this text, Jesus challenged His followers to have faith as a "seed." Jesus is called the "Seed" (Gen. 3:15); the Word of God is designated as "seed" (Luke 8:11; 1 Pet. 1:23); the growth of the believer is likened to a plant (John 15); and the evangelism of the world to a harvest (Matt. 13:30). This only begins the imagery of "seed faith" in the Bible.

It is altogether desirable to capture a firm grasp of this truth, the essence of which is that the little we have to bring to God is not a limit to faith's possibilities. When we bring Him the smallest of our strength, our resource, and our ability, and place it in His hands—sown like a seed—there is a guaranteed fruitfulness and harvest forthcoming.

Is there anything in your life that you hesitate to place in His hands? Do not fear! He is faithful and He guarantees an abundant harvest!

Increasing Faith

Protection

Above all, [take] the shield of faith with which you will be able to quench all the fiery darts of the wicked one.   *Ephesians 6:16*

First Peter 5:8 says that our "adversary the devil walks about like a roaring lion, seeking whom he may devour." His attack against us is relentless as he seeks to tempt us (Matt. 4:1), oppose us (Zech. 3:1), bring disease (Job 2:7), and prompt us to sin (Acts 5:3). In fact, John 10:10 says that all of Satan's efforts are aimed at causing three things: robbery, death, and destruction.

But we have not been left without defense!

This text challenges us to take up the shield of faith! The Greek word for "faith" literally means "conviction, confidence, trust, belief." But what are we to have our confidence in? The Lord. Psalm 3:3 says, "But You, O Lord, are a shield for me." This psalm later speaks of God not only defending us, but pursuing our enemies and saving us from the enemies' snare through rescue (v. 4), rest (v. 5), and deliverance (v. 6).

Rest in that promise today. Our shield of faith is the Lord!

The Family

Marriage—Part 1

But I want you to know that the head of every man is Christ, the head of woman is man, and the head of Christ is God.

1 Corinthians 11:3

The relationship between God as "head" and Christ as Son is a model for the relationship between husband and wife. It provides us with principles that can be applied within the marriage relationship.

We are to share a mutual love (John 5:20; 14:31), live in unity (John 10:30; 14:9, 11), and hold one another in highest esteem (John 8:49, 54). In the description of the virtuous wife of Proverbs 31, the writer noted that the husband rose up and called his wife blessed and that he praised her (Prov. 31:28). To honor, to hold in esteem, and praise your mate builds an unshakable trust in each other. Husbands are also to care for their wives (Eph. 5:28), while wives are to exercise authority entrusted to them with humility and without competition (Phil. 2:3).

As we follow the principles illustrated in Jesus and the Father's relationship, we will see our marriages built up in faith, impenetrable to the enemy's devices, and extending ministry in Jesus' Name.

The Family

Marriage—Part 2

*I will make you swear by the Lord, the God of heaven and the
God of the earth, that you will not take a wife for my son from
the daughters of the Canaanites.*
            Genesis 24:3

*I*n his last days, Abraham's primary concern was that
his son should marry a woman of the same faith. The
servant obeyed his master and, with the Lord's guidance,
found Rebekah as a wife for Isaac.

The command to marry only within their faith was repeated to Israel throughout the Old Testament (Deut. 7:3;
Neh. 13:25). The consequences of intermarriages were
devastating. The scriptural report of Solomon, who married many foreign wives, was "that his wives turned his
heart after other gods; and his heart was not loyal to the
Lord" (1 Kin. 11:1, 4). The theme continues in the New
Testament: "Do not be unequally yoked together with
unbelievers" (2 Cor. 6:14).

We no longer live in a culture where parents arrange their
children's marriages. But we can pray. The prayers for a
godly husband or wife should begin the day our children
are born so that as they enter marriage they will have partners in faith who will strengthen their hearts in the Lord.

The Family

One Flesh

And the two shall become one flesh.   *Mark 10:8*

One day the Pharisees tested Jesus on the subject of divorce. In answer, He rehearsed the story of the creation and union of male and female: "For this reason a man shall leave his father and mother and be joined to his wife, and the two shall become one flesh; so then they are no longer two, but one flesh" (Mark 10:7, 8).

The marriage union was ordained by God. From the beginning man was instructed to leave his family so that he could be joined to his wife. The Greek word for "join" means "to glue or cement together, stick to, adhere to, join firmly." The joining together of a man and a woman in marriage implies permanency. The fact that God joined them together reinforces the concept (Mark 10:9).

When the two become one, unity is established—unity in spirit and in flesh. The God-witnessed union is to remain through joy and adversity, with husband and wife committed to each other and to their Creator.

Build on the Rock

Unless the Lord builds the house, they labor in vain who build it.
Psalm 127:1

uilding your dream house is an exciting project. From the planning and design to watching the building go up, to decorating and moving in—all are a part of making it just the way you want it. We all put a lot of thought into our homes, but this Scripture tells us we have a more permanent residence.

God the master builder knows how to build our spiritual homes. He is the architect. He drew the blueprints. His design is perfect and eternal. When we try to build our homes or our families without consulting the chief architect, our labor is in vain. But when we work with Him in the construction process, when we consult His blueprints— the Word of God—and seek His advice in prayer, the result is enduring.

Jesus said, "Whoever hears these sayings of Mine, and does them, I will liken him to a wise man who built his house on the rock" (Matt. 7:24). As we build our homes on God's Word, our house will stand when others fall, because its foundation is solidly built on Jesus Christ Himself.

The Family

Heirs Together

Husbands, likewise, dwell with them with understanding . . . and as being heirs together of the grace of life, that your prayers may not be hindered.   *1 Peter 3:7*

This passage of Scripture opens with a command to wives to live their lives in such a Christ-like manner that their unbelieving husbands will be irresistibly drawn to Christ (3:1). It concludes by encouraging husbands to understand and honor their wives.

Peter goes on to say that when we do not live in understanding and honor, our own relationship with God can be hampered and our prayers go unanswered. It is when our lives reflect Jesus' actions and attitudes that the channel to God is opened wide. Our spiritual health and growth is assured, and we become "heirs together of the grace of life." The word "heir" denotes a joint participant, or one who receives a lot or a possession with another.

Our godly inheritance is "the grace of life," a fruitful life here and for eternity with the Lord. Now He calls us, along with our spouse, to be joint participants in our purpose and joint recipients of His promise.

Ears to Hear

The Lord came and stood and called as at other times . . . And
Samuel answered, "Speak, for Your servant hears."

1 Samuel 3:10

*A*an early age Samuel had a heart for the Lord and ears sensitive to His voice. He "ministered before the Lord, even as a child" (1 Sam. 2:18).

As parents we must teach our children to have spiritually sensitive ears that can discern the Lord's voice. Jesus repeatedly cried out, "He who has ears to hear, let him hear!" (Matt. 11:15; 13:43; Mark 4:23; Luke 8:8). Elijah learned to hear God's "still small voice" (1 Kin. 19:12). The Apostle Paul's life was changed in a moment when he heard the voice of the Lord (Acts 9:4), and he simultaneously received salvation and direction for his life.

We can teach our children how to hear God's voice by sharing with them times that we have heard His voice and how we responded. God speaks to us in many ways as we go through each day. Let us ask the Lord to give us ears sensitive to hear His voice and wisdom to teach those same lessons to our children.

The Family

Love Without Partiality

And Isaac loved Esau because he ate of his game, but Rebekah loved Jacob.   *Genesis 25:28*

God had blessed Isaac and Rebekah with twin sons. As the boys grew, they developed very different interests. Esau became a hunter, a real outdoorsman, and this appealed to Isaac. Jacob worked in the fields closer to home, so he spent much of his time with Rebekah. The partiality of their parents soon became obvious. Esau is even referred to as "his" (Isaac's) son (Gen. 27:5) and Jacob as "her" (Rebekah's) son (Gen. 27:6). This partiality became a curse within the family, bringing deception and division.

Partiality has no place in our families. It will hurt, divide, and destroy relationships. As parents, we should follow God's example: "God shows no partiality" (Acts 10:34).

Partiality means "to take sides, show favoritism, show discrimination, treat one person better than another." God's love and grace are available for all, without partiality, and we should love our children the same way. As they grow and learn to rest securely in our love, they will learn to rest just as securely in the Father's love.

Don't Give Up

Now Eli was very old; and he heard everything his sons did to all Israel, and how they lay with the women who assembled at the door of the tabernacle of meeting.   1 Samuel 2:22

What went wrong with these sons of a godly priest? Scripture tells us that while Eli ministered before the Lord, his sons were "corrupt" and their sins were "very great" (1 Sam. 2:12,17).

We do not know everything that brought Eli's sons to this appalling circumstance, but we do know that they did not know the Lord (1 Sam. 2:12), and that they did not have any regard for their father's warning to repent (1 Sam. 2:25). Twice Eli was warned that destruction would come to his household because of his sons' sins, but Eli's response was despondent. "Let [the Lord] do what seems good to Him" (1 Sam. 3:18). Eli had given up.

We have promise regarding our children's salvation (Prov. 22:6), but we also have a God-given charge to instruct them in the knowledge of the Lord.

Do not give up! Even when the situation looks grim, let the Lord's unfailing love flow through you to them, drawing them into the family of the redeemed.

The Family

Dedicating Our Children

Therefore I also have lent him to the Lord; as long as he lives he shall be lent to the Lord.   *1 Samuel 1:28*

One of the most difficult lessons that parents have to learn is to hold their children with open hands because they belong to the Lord. Hannah is the ultimate picture of the "open-handed" parent. She had vowed that she would give her son back to the Lord "all the days of his life" (1 Sam. 1:11). Hannah fulfilled her promise by bringing her son Samuel to live and serve in the tabernacle. The word "lent" used here means to give unconditionally in dedication to the Lord.

In Luke 2, we see another example of parents giving their child to the Lord when Mary and Joseph present the infant Jesus at the temple in Jerusalem. In doing this, they were not only affirming God's prior claim on the child's life, but committing themselves to raise him in God's ways.

We as parents should follow the same example in dedicating our children to the Lord. How God chooses to use them is not for us to decide, but He allows us to partner with Him in directing our children toward His purpose.

The Family

Little Blessings

Children are a heritage from the Lord, the fruit of the womb is a reward.   Psalm 127:3

The Creator's words to the newly created man and woman were, "Be fruitful and multiply" (Gen. 1:28). Children are the result of that command. The verse in Psalms tells us that children are "a heritage from the Lord." We inherit them from God Himself. He entrusts them to us just as one would entrust a fortune to the heirs.

Children are also referred to as a reward. A reward is something that is given in return for something done. At the time children are given to parents they are really unearned. It is in loving and caring for our children and in seeing them mature in the Lord that the reward comes.

The world promotes a totally different attitude toward children. They are viewed as burdens rather than blessings. The next time we are tempted to frustration with our children, let us remember that Scripture promises, "Children's children are the crown of old men" (Prov. 17:6). God's reward is perpetual; it continues for generations!

The Family

Teach Your Children—Part 1

And these words which I command you today shall be in your heart. You shall teach them diligently to your children.

Deuteronomy 6:6, 7

One of our primary responsibilities as parents is to teach our children the way of the Lord. Scripture tells us that this should be a constant and ongoing process: "[You] shall talk of them when you sit in your house, when you walk by the way, when you lie down, and when you rise up" (v. 7).

Jesus said that the law hung on two commandments: love the Lord God and love your neighbor (Matt. 22:27–40). The words He quoted come immediately before the command given here to teach our children. "You shall love the Lord your God with all your heart, with all your soul, and with all your strength" (Deut. 6:5). This is what we are to impart to our children above all else.

What are we teaching our children? Are we living in such a way that our children will be drawn to the Lord? May our words and our actions bring honor to the Lord and life to our children as we lead them in His ways.

Teach Your Children—Part 2

And you, fathers, do not provoke your children to wrath, but bring them up in the training and admonition of the Lord.

Ephesians 6:4

What a contrast! Provoking our children to wrath versus bringing them up in the training and admonition of the Lord. The pivotal point is crucial—we are either turning our children away from God or toward God. That puts great responsibility on us as parents!

In a home where anger, condemnation, sarcasm, intimidation, and fear rule, there is no love manifested, and children will be "turned off" to God and "turned on" to wrath. The same traits that we exhibit in our lives will soon be seen in them.

But in a home where there is peace, encouragement, patience, consistency, joy, diligence, and love, children learn of the Lord naturally because they see God's characteristics lived out in front of them. A firm spiritual foundation can be established for children to grow in their knowledge and understanding of the Lord.

Paul wrote of Timothy, "from childhood you have known the Holy Scriptures, which are able to make you wise for salvation through faith which is in Christ Jesus" (2 Tim. 3:15). May the same be true of our children.

The Family

Teach Your Children—Part 3

But whoever causes one of these little ones who believe in Me to sin, it would be better for him if a millstone were hung around his neck, and he were drowned in the depth of the sea.

Matthew 18:6

Jesus sharply rebuked His disciples when they tried to stop parents from bringing their children to Him: "He was greatly displeased and said to them, 'Let the little children come to Me, and do not forbid them; for of such is the kingdom of God.' . . . And He took them up in His arms, laid His hands on them, and blessed them" (Mark 10:14, 16). Their value to the Lord is great!

According to the psalmist, children are a heritage from the Lord (Ps. 127:3). Scripture repeatedly reminds parents to love, teach, discipline, and protect their children (Eph. 6:4; Deut. 6:6, 7; Prov. 13:24; Heb. 12:11). This warning to those who would cause a child to sin is severe, but it is a reminder of our responsibility before the Lord for our children.

We as parents must guard our words and actions so that we never cause our children to stumble or sin. Rather, out of our love for them, everything that we do and say must reflect God's love, God's Word, and God's ways (Deut. 6:6. 7).

Teach Your Children—Part 4

Then Pharaoh's daughter said to her, "Take this child away and nurse him for me, and I will give you your wages." So the woman took the child and nursed him.   Exodus 2:9

Moses' parents obviously took advantage of the short time they had to teach their son about their God.

They had defied Pharaoh's command to throw their new-born son into the river. Instead, they hid him for three months and then placed him in a small basket among the reeds along the river's bank. Miracle of miracles happened when Pharaoh's daughter found the infant and unknow-ingly called on his mother to be his nurse. After several years, he was returned to Pharaoh's daughter as her son.

Moses' parents must have done a thorough job! The writer of Hebrews tells us that, though raised in Pharaoh's court, Moses, upon reaching manhood, chose to suffer affliction with God's people rather than to enjoy the pleasures of sin and the treasures in Egypt (Heb. 11:25, 26).

Our time with our children is short. How are we doing? Will the spiritual training we provide be adequate? Let us pray that the lessons we teach our children will sink deep into their hearts and make them strong to resist the world's enticements.

The Family

Joy

I will rejoice in the Lord, I will joy in the God of my salvation.
Habakkuk 3:18

The word "joy" means to rejoice and be glad. The Hebrew word for joy contains the suggestion of "dancing or leaping for joy, spinning around with intense motion." What brings this kind of joy to an individual, a marriage, or a family—the kind of joy that would cause one to dance, leap, and spin around? Is it our possessions, our jobs, even our friends or family?

The prophet Habakkuk looked around and saw the devastating results of the Babylonian invasion. He concluded that he could be stripped of everything and his joy would still be there! He had learned that joy does not come from things which can be so quickly lost, but eternal joy comes from the Lord, the God of our salvation.

What a lesson for us who get so easily caught up with jobs, possessions, and the problems of the present moment. Are our children learning to live in the stress of the world or the joy of the Lord? Teach them. Pick them up and dance, leap, spin around. Proclaim the joy of God and His salvation!

Discipline in Love

He who spares his rod hates his son, but he who loves him disciplines him promptly.   Proverbs 13:24

Discipline is the other side of teaching. A child with a teachable spirit will still need thorough explanation, much patience, and opportunity to try and experiment, including the right to fail and to learn by failure. A child, however, who is caught up in willful disobedience (Prov. 29:15), rebellion (1 Sam. 15:23), or stubborn foolishness (Prov. 22:15), closes off effective teaching and disrupts the harmony of the family. God's answer to this is firm and loving discipline.

The Bible makes a clear distinction between discipline and physical abuse. We are never to inflict harm on a child (Prov. 23:13), but at times pain may be a part of effective correction.

God describes Himself as a strict disciplinarian. He always disciplines us out of love and for our own benefit (Heb. 12:5–11). Likewise, God requires that parents properly correct their children. Discipline drives foolishness from a child's heart (Prov. 29:15), gives wisdom (Prov. 29:15), and produces righteousness in the child's life (Heb. 12:11). Even a child's eternal destiny can hinge upon the godly discipline provided by parents (Prov. 23:14).

The Family

Rest

It is vain for you to rise up early, to sit up late, to eat the bread of sorrows; for so He gives His beloved sleep.   **Psalm 127:2**

Though he wrote twenty-five hundred years ago, the writer of this psalm obviously had experienced the "rat race." The theme is appropriate for today. Husbands and wives keep a frantic pace just to keep their family financially solvent. They rise early and rush off to the office. They work long hours, and when they finally arrive back home, they are too exhausted to sleep. So they sit up late, usually in front of the television, until at last sleep comes. Meaningful dialogue is nonexistent. The focus is on the job, not home, on the paycheck, not relationships. For what? Solomon knew the answer: nothing. The bread of their labor is sorrow.

But God "gives His beloved sleep." When we follow God's way, we do not have to get caught up in this "rat race," for God will provide what we need, and He can do it so that we have meaningful time with our families. Then the bread of our labor can become joy, not sorrow, and we can rest, not run.

His Workmanship

You formed my inward parts; You covered me in my mother's womb.

Psalm 139:13

We all need reassurance about who we are. Doubts arise. Who am I? Why am I here? This may be even more true of our children.

Reading the above words of the psalmist can bring confidence, assurance, and self-worth. It is God who made us. His handiwork began in the womb where He skillfully wove our white bones, blue veins, and red arteries into a beautiful embroidery. The thought is repeated in verse 15 where "wrought" means "embroidered with various colors." His finished work is awesome, wonderful, marvelous.

The Apostle Paul later wrote, "We are His workmanship, created in Christ Jesus for good works" (Eph. 2:10). The word "workmanship" comes from the Greek word *poiema*, which means "that which is manufactured, a product, a design produced by an artisan." It emphasizes God as the master architect, the Creator of the universe, and the Creator of man. We are His workmanship; we were formed by the master designer Himself, and marvelous are His works.

The Family

Serve the Lord

Choose for yourselves this day whom you will serve . . . But as for me and my house, we will serve the Lord.   Joshua 24:15

Near the end of his life, the great warrior Joshua addressed the children of Israel. Now that they were in the Promised Land, they would have to decide where their spiritual allegiance would lie—with the God of their fathers or the gods of their newly conquered land. With boldness Joshua proclaimed that he had made his choice—he and his family would serve the Lord.

Every couple must make this decision for their families. It not only determines their future, but also that of their children. To choose to serve the Lord will bring peace and blessing to the family both now and in the future. "All your children shall be taught by the Lord, and great shall be the peace of your children" (Is. 54:13). "The righteous man walks in his integrity; his children are blessed after him" (Prov. 20:7). The influence goes even beyond our children to our "children's children" (Ps. 103:17) and our "descendants' descendants" (Is. 59:21).

Choose for yourselves this day whom you will serve. And let that choice be to serve the Lord.

Our Refuge

In the fear of the Lord there is strong confidence, and His children will have a place of refuge.   Proverbs 14:26

The word "refuge" occurs twenty times in the Old Testament. It is defined as "a shelter, or protection, fortress; a place of trust; a shelter from storm."

The writers of the Scriptures often used the image of God as being their refuge. "The eternal God is your refuge" (Deut. 33:27), promised Moses. "God is our refuge and strength, a very present help in trouble" (Ps. 46:1), wrote the psalmist. And the prophet Isaiah described God as being "a refuge from the storm" (Is. 25:4).

Godly families of today are not immune to the storms of life, which seem to move in frequently, often without warning. The present storm may be sickness, heartache caused by a wayward child, a financial setback, the death of a friend, or a broken relationship. But His children still have a place of refuge, a shelter from the storm.

Like the faithful of long ago, we must pass on to our children our confidence in the Lord, so that they, too, will be able to weather the storms of life after they leave the shelter of home.

The Family

Hearts of Love

But when he was still a great way off, his father saw him and had compassion, and ran and fell on his neck and kissed him.

Luke 15:20

The parable of the lost son is one of the most moving stories in all of Scripture. It is a story of folly, repentance, compassion, and forgiveness. After reaching the depths of sin, the runaway son comes to his senses and remembers his father. There is only one thing to do—return home and beg forgiveness.

In the meantime, the father's love has not diminished. Daily he scans the horizon for his wayward son. And then one day it happens—his son appears in the distance. The father runs to him, and as the son begins to confess his sins, the father interrupts and calls for a celebration (Luke 15:24).

The point is clear. This is the story of our return to our compassionate heavenly Father. "But God demonstrates His own love toward us, in that while we were still sinners, Christ died for us" (Rom. 5:8). It, too, is a promise for parents and their unbelieving children. In spite of their sin may we always have hearts of love, compassion, and forgiveness that allow them to return.

The Family

Imitate Christ

Imitate me, just as I also imitate Christ.   *1 Corinthians 11:1*

Paul's life matched his words to such an extent that he could make this bold statement! And those who imitated his life became more like Christ.

As parents, we should follow Christ so closely that we can say to our children, "Imitate me as I imitate Christ." We are our children's first and most closely observed role model. This does not mean that we have to be perfect. But our lives should be open before them to see all of what Jesus does in us as we rely on His strength for our obedience and His redemption for our failures.

In his letter to the Philippians Paul wrote, "The things which you learned and received and heard and saw in me, these do, and the God of peace will be with you" (Phil. 4:9). What have our children learned and received from us? What have they heard us say? What have they seen us do? If we are imitating Christ, they will have learned, received, heard, and seen Him. And the promise is that God's peace will be in their hearts.

The Family

Obedience

Children, obey your parents in the Lord, for this is right.
Ephesians 6:1

Obedience is a trait that we as parents should instill in our children at a very early age. The lessons usually begin for their protection and safety: "Don't touch the hot stove," or "Don't go into the street." As children grow, obedience to our word should become second nature, and they should begin to obey out of love and trust for us.

The word "obey" comes from the Greek word *hupakauo,* which means "to hear as a subordinate, listen attentively, obey as a subject, answer and respond, and submit without reservation." The word contains the ideas of hearing, responding, and obeying.

Paul concludes this verse by saying, "for this is right." The Greek word for "right" is *dikaious,* which implies "conforming to the laws of God and man." By teaching our children to obey our words, we are teaching them to obey God and His Word. And it is that obedience that matters for eternity.

Honor Your Parents

Honor your father and mother . . . that it may be well with you
and you may live long on the earth.   *Ephesians 6:2, 3*

In this text, Paul charges children to show honor to their parents. To honor means "to prize highly, or to show respect."

We cannot teach our children to honor or respect us; it must be earned. As our children, who are our closest observers, watch our lives and listen to our words, their respect for us will either grow or diminish. Their attitude toward us will be molded by what they see us do and hear us say. They will learn to respect others by seeing how we respect others. They will see how we relate to our parents and act accordingly. If we treat our parents with honor, they will learn that the command to honor them is a life-time command; it does not end when we move away and begin our families.

By earning the respect of our children and by giving honor to our own parents, we will all become recipients of God's promise, and it will "be well with [us] and [we will] live long on the earth."

The Family

Finding Direction

Trust in the Lord with all your heart, and lean not on your own
understanding; in all your ways acknowledge Him, and He shall
direct your paths.   Proverbs 3:5, 6

This text gives a three-pronged course of action for guiding our children toward God's plan for their lives.

First, they must trust in the Lord with all of their heart. That trust will be determined by how we have taught and lived *our* trust in Him. Our trust must be equally as whole-hearted if we are to pass that characteristic on to the next generation.

Next, they cannot depend on their own understanding to figure out God's way for their lives. God's way cannot always be rationalized because His ways are higher than our ways (Is. 55:8, 9). Helping our children learn to hear God's voice for themselves opens the door to trusting Him even when it doesn't make sense.

Third, we must teach our children to acknowledge God in all they do. "Acknowledge" suggests that one should be fully aware of and in fellowship with the Lord.

The result will be sure direction. The word "direct" suggests that God will straighten out the path of His servants. That is what we want for ourselves and our children.

The Family

Training

Train up a child in the way he should go, and when he is old he will not depart from it.   Proverbs 22:6

Often we think that if our children just watch our walk with Christ it will naturally rub off on them. We *do* need to be aware of what our children see lived out in us, but God demands more of us in preparing our children for life. He calls us to train them.

To "train up" requires that parents impart wisdom, love, nurture, and discipline to their children so that they become fully equipped and committed to the Lord. "In the way he should go" implies that the training should be according to the unique personality, gifts, and aspirations of each child. It also means that children should be taught to avoid any of their natural tendencies that might prevent them from making a total commitment to Christ.

In order for training to be effective, children must put into practice what they are taught. Opportunities to demonstrate their spiritual skills must be given them so that when the real challenges come they will pass the test—both now and for a lifetime.

The Family

On Money

The love of money is a root of all kinds of evil, for which some have strayed from the faith.   1 Timothy 6:10

The Bible clearly teaches that misusing money can lead to physical, moral, and spiritual decay. This text indicates that loving money is the source of all kinds of evil, that it can cause individuals to stray from their faith and that it can bring many sorrows. The previous verse states that those who desire to be rich fall into temptations, snares, and foolish and harmful lusts which lead to destruction.

These are solemn warnings, and we must take note of them. And we must train our children so that they learn to keep money in proper perspective. We must teach them to tithe and give offerings as the basis for their financial security (Mal. 3:7–10). Scripture further elaborates on such practical issues as saving (Prov. 21:20), controlling debt (Prov. 22:7), and giving to the poor and needy (Prov. 22:9).

Teaching our children to become faithful stewards financially becomes the foundation for them to learn how to give their lives in love to the Lord and in ministry to the world.

Protection and Trust

Have You not made a hedge around him, around his household, and around all that he has on every side?   Job 1:10

The interrogator was Satan. The one being questioned was God. The subject of the conversation was Job, who was described as a man who "was blameless and upright, and one who feared God and shunned evil" (Job 1:1). Satan contended that if God's protective hedge were removed Job would no longer serve the Lord but would curse Him. Satan was wrong. After being stripped of family and possessions, Job proclaimed, "Though He slay me, yet will I trust Him" (Job 13:15).

During the few brief years that our children are in our safekeeping, we must teach them to trust in the Lord. There comes a time when we can no longer be with them constantly, and it is then that we must pray God will keep them from the wiles of the adversary (Eph. 6:11).

As our children grow in the Lord, first under our protection and then under God's protection, they will come to know His presence and, like Job, trust in Him unreservedly.

The Family

God's Mighty Deeds

We will not hide them from their children, telling to the genera-
tion to come the praises of the Lord, and His strength and His
wonderful works that He has done.   Psalm 78:4

The Old Testament frequently exhorts us to recount to our children God's faithfulness and mighty works. The Lord instructed Moses to "tell in the hearing of your son and your son's son the mighty things I have done in Egypt" (Ex. 10:2). Moses told the children of Israel to teach "the things your eyes have seen . . . to your children and your grandchildren" (Deut. 4:9). Our children need to hear these things so "that they may set their hope in God, and not forget the works of God, but keep His command-ments" (Ps. 78:7).

God continues to do wondrous things, and we must share them with our children. As we rehearse to our children the power of God that saved, that healed, that provided for, that protected us and our families, they, too, will set their hope in God. Their faith will be strengthened, and they will stand firm in the Lord, knowing that He will answer them as well when they have need.

The Family

The Word

Your word I have hidden in my heart, that I might not sin against You.

                                                    Psalm 119:11

Psalm 119 exalts the Word of the Lord like no other passage in Scripture. The Word is referred to in every verse and is referred to by many different names: the Law, commandments, testimonies, statutes, precepts, judgments, ordinance, Word, and way.

The benefits of the Word are numerous. "Those who keep His testimonies . . . do no iniquity" (vv. 2, 3). His statutes prevent shame (v. 6), and sin (v. 11), and can be our song (v. 54). His testimonies bring delight (v. 24). His Word revives (v. 25), strengthens (v. 28), and cleanses (v. 9); brings salvation (v. 41) and mercy (v. 58); gives life (v. 50) and hope (v. 74); and keeps us from straying (v. 67). His commandments give understanding (v. 73). And that is only the beginning!

There is no greater gift that we can give to our children than a thirst, an appreciation, and a love for God's Word. As our children store up God's Word in their hearts, it will give them sure footing for life: "I thought about my ways, and turned my feet to Your testimonies. I . . . did not delay to keep Your commandments" (vv. 59, 60).

The Family

The Pathway of Praise

Purposeful Praise

Enter into His gates with thanksgiving, and into His courts with praise.　　　　　　　　　　　　　　　　　　*Psalm 100:4*

Man was created to live and breathe in an atmosphere of praise-filled worship to His Creator. The avenue of sustained inflow of divine power to man was to be kept open by the sustained outflow of joyous and humble praise to his Maker.

The severance of the bond of blessing-through-obedience that sin brought silenced man's praise-filled fellowship with God and introduced self-centeredness, self-pitying, and complaint (see Gen. 3:9–12). But upon receiving salvation and life through Christ, daily living calls us to prayer and the Word for fellowship and wisdom in living.

Our daily approach to God in that communion is to be paved with praise: "Enter into His gates with thanksgiving, and into His courts with praise." Such a walk of praise-filled openness to Him will cultivate deep devotion, faithful obedience, and constant joy.

We can move into each day that we live knowing that a praise-walk is not fanatical and glib, nor reduced to mere ritual; but a walk of life-delivering power is available to those of us who believe in Jesus.

Pathway of Praise

Dry Times

Then Israel sang this song: "Spring up, O well! All of you sing to it—"
           Numbers 21:17

raise is a cure for the "dry times" that come to every believer. Here, in Israel's wilderness wanderings, praise to God caused waters to flow from a well. God gave the people both instruction and promise: "Gather together, and I will give water." As they gathered in the unity and power that attends a corporate meeting, they saw God fulfill His promise to bring life—sustaining water from the well. The people's responsibility was simply to sing and watch God work His miracle.

In times of pressure, anxiety, or depression, we are not to stay alone. We gather with God's people, especially His praising people. Regardless of our personal feelings, let us join in audible praise and sing to our well—the living God who supplies all our need. Let our song be one of thanksgiving for past blessings and of faith in God's promises for the present and for the future.

Like Israel, let us sing in our "dry places," and watch as God overflows us with His bountiful blessings.

Victory in Praise

Now when they began to sing and to praise, the Lord set ambushes against the people of Ammon, Moab, and Mount Seir, who had come out against Judah; and they were defeated.

2 Chronicles 20:22

Here is a great lesson on the power of praise. Judah was confronted by mortal enemies, Moab and Ammon. The people sought God in prayer and with faith in His Word (2 Chr. 20:1–14). Then came the prophet's word: "Do not be afraid . . . for the battle is not yours, but God's" (v. 15).

The victory came in a strange but powerful manner. The Levites stood and praised "the Lord God of Israel with voices loud and high" (v. 19). Then some of them were appointed to precede the army as they headed into the battle and, as they went, they were to sing to the Lord and praise Him in the beauty of holiness.

The result of this powerful praise was total victory! As they began to sing and to praise God with the expectancy that He would fight for them, the enemies were defeated. This incident is not unique, but has parallels in other Old Testament victories (see Josh. 6:10, 20; Judg. 7:18–22; 2 Kin. 7:3–16; 19:35). Whenever and wherever God's people praise Him, He reigns among them and does miraculous things on their behalf.

Pathway of Praise

Triumphant Praise

Paul and Silas were praying and singing hymns to God, and . . .
suddenly there was a great earthquake . . . and everyone's chains
were loosed.   Acts 16:25, 26

This text is an example of the power of praise, even in difficult circumstances. Beaten and imprisoned, Paul and Silas respond by singing a hymn of praise—a song sung directly from the heart to God. The relationship between their song of praise and their supernatural deliverance through the earthquake cannot be overlooked. Praise directed toward God can shake open prison doors! A man was converted, his household saved, and satanic captivity overthrown in Philippi.

And this is not the only example of triumphant praise in Scripture. Look at Gideon as he leads his band of soldiers into battle with the shout, "The sword of the Lord!" (Judg. 7:1–22). Jehoshaphat put the worshipers in front of his army as they marched into battle (2 Chr. 20:1–24). And David, the "sweet psalmist of Israel," repeatedly intertwined the themes of praise and victory (Ps. 9:1–3; 28:7–9; 71:8–11; 142:6, 7).

Today, as well, praise will cause every chain of bondage to drop away. When you are serving God and things do not go the way you planned, learn from these examples. Praise triumphs gloriously!

Pathway of Praise

Christian Community—Part 1

Breaking bread from house to house, they ate their food with gladness and simplicity of heart, praising God and having favor with all the people.   Acts 2:46, 47

The church of Jesus Christ may be defined as a *worshipping* community. One of the most fundamental and foundational acts of God's people is worship. Because God does what He does—saves, heals, restores, renews, refreshes—we do what we do—praise, adore, give thanks, worship. To the God who has called us to Himself we respond in worship, obedience, and service.

In our relationship with God we get our definition: We are the people of God, and because we are His, we worship. By worshipping the one true God, we become true persons; by this act we fulfill our ultimate destiny. Many aspects of this life will be left behind when we enter the next world, but one thing will remain: through all eternity we will continue to worship the Lord who redeemed us in love and His Christ who saved us by grace.

Today also we commit ourselves to be people of praise. In doing so we link ourselves with the worshipping community in this world and in the next.

Pathway of Praise

Christian Community—Part 2

So continuing daily with one accord . . . praising God and having favor with all the people. Acts 2:46, 47

The people of God worship, and when we do, we worship together. Thus, the church forms a worshipping community. Our primary meaning comes from our relationship with God as people who worship Him. But part of our meaning comes from our relationship with others as the community worships together.

Our life together is based on shared worship. We discover that what is true of the whole church is true of all its parts. Each segment of the church gains its reality as community when its members worship. Husbands and wives find a new dimension of oneness as they worship together. Parents who pray with their children strengthen already existing ties. Small groups, committees, boards, and task forces move beyond natural affinity and shared work to supernatural unity as they commit themselves to worship together. The choir preparing to lead the congregation in praise discovers a new measure of harmony when part of their preparation is shared worship.

Thus we gladly rejoice with one another and experience the tie that binds our hearts in Christian love.

Bless the Lord

Every day I will bless You, and I will praise Your name forever and ever. Psalm 145:2

*D*avid's declaration is that he will bless God each day that he lives.

How do we bless God? Isn't He always the "Blesser" and we always the "blessees"? The two ideas of giving and receiving a blessing are brought together in the word David uses here for "bless," in Hebrew *barach,* which is derived from *berech,* "knee." In Old Testament times, one got down on his knees when preparing to speak or receive words of blessing.

From God's side, He is the Blesser, the One who gives the capacity for living a full, rich life. The Creator's first act toward the newly created man and woman was to bless them (Gen. 1:28). The Aaronic Benediction (Num. 6:22–27) reaffirms God's continuing promise of blessing to His people.

From our side, we kneel before our Creator God and receive His enabling power to live this day in peace, equipped for every eventuality by His provision. Then, also from our knees, we respond to His blessing by lifting our words of praise and thanks to Him.

Pathway of Praise

A Chosen Generation

You are a chosen generation, a royal priesthood, a holy nation,
His own special people, that you may proclaim the praises of Him
who called you.   *1 Peter 2:9*

This text not only appoints praise but represents a basic revelation of the Bible: God wants a people who will walk with Him in prayer, march with Him in praise, and thank and worship Him. In Peter's description, notice how the people of the New Covenant are to progress.

First, we are called a chosen generation—a people begun with Jesus' choice of the Twelve, who became 120, to whom were added thousands at Pentecost. We are a part of this continually expanding generation, "chosen" when we receive Christ. Then we are a royal priesthood. Under the Old Covenant the priesthood and royalty were separated. In Christ we are now "kings and priests" (Rev. 1:6), prepared for walking with Him in the light or warring beside Him against the hosts of darkness. Next He makes us a holy nation, born of Jesus' blood, from every nation under heaven.

Finally He calls us His own special people. God's intention has always been to call forth a people who will proclaim His praise and propagate His blessing throughout the earth. Let us do that today.

Pathway of Praise

His Eminence

The Lord is high above all nations, His glory above the heavens.
Psalm 113:4

"*E*minence" refers to the high position of God. "Who is a God like You?" asks the prophet Micah (7:18). He gets no response; there is no one like God.

God is far above all people on earth. Consider the power that may rest in one person, a general, a king, or a president. God is far above him in power. "Who is like the Lord our God, who dwells on high, who humbles Himself to behold the things that are in the heavens and in the earth?" (Ps. 113:5, 6). Our exalted Lord looks down from His throne, not just on earth, but on the heavens.

Here, then, is reason to praise the Lord. He is not bound to our boundaries nor tied by our time. His resources are unlimited, His power and authority unequalled. The authority of a king stops at the border of his nation. The power of a general reaches only as far as the number of his tanks and planes. So, "Praise the Lord!" for His perspective is right and His might is abundant.

His Immanence

He raises the poor out of the dust, and lifts the needy out of the ash heap.
                                              Psalm 113:7

God's "immanence" refers to His coming to dwell among men. This is the heart of the Bible. God has come down; the Word has become flesh. The Creator God in heaven is the Redeemer God come to earth. The Lord who is seated on high (v. 5) is the same Lord who reaches into the dust. The Lord whose glory is above the heavens (v. 4) is the same Lord who lifts the needy from the ash heap.

The word here for "needy" has a technical meaning. It does not simply refer to one who has no money, but to one who, lacking the world's resources, comes to put his trust in God who becomes his help. If we are poor and needy, we praise God, for He is looking for people like that to lift and restore. He is not so far above us that He cannot reach us where we are. He is seated on high, but He looks down and sees us. Thus, we worship Him.

Bless the Lord

Bless the Lord, O my soul, and forget not all His benefits.

Psalm 103:2

Blessing God is remembering His kindness and recognizing that He is the Giver of all good things. He forgives, heals, redeems, crowns, satisfies, and strengthens (vv. 3–5). Psalm 103 concludes with the same exhortation it began with: "Bless the Lord, O my soul!"

From the "Bless the Lord" in verse 1 to the "Bless the Lord" in v. 22, the psalmist broadened his vision considerably. In verse 1 praise flows out of a context of personal well-being resulting from God's deliverance. In verse 22 worship rises from the knowledge of God's universal rule, for "His kingdom rules over all" (v. 19). So what began with an individual has combined with all creation's mighty chorus of praise to the Lord.

Bless the Lord, all you His hosts,
You ministers of His, who do His pleasure.
Bless the Lord, all His works,
In all places of His dominion.
Bless the Lord, O my soul!

The amazing fact is that the voice of the psalmist is not lost to God in such thunderous praise! Let us join in the chorus.

Pathway of Praise

Togetherness

Be filled with the Spirit, speaking to one another in psalms and hymns and spiritual songs, singing and making melody in your heart to the Lord.   Ephesians 5:18, 19

When the Spirit-filled church worships she constantly gives thanks. Everything that comes to believers is a cause for thanksgiving. Thanks to God comes to a focus in Christ; He is God's supreme Gift to the church. In His name, because of what God the Father said to the world through His Son Jesus Christ, God's people find reason to rejoice in everything that happens (v. 20). The Spirit-filled church worships God in the name of Jesus Christ.

The Spirit-filled church worships God together. The Spirit has brought a unity and a communion among them. They speak to each other and then speak together to God. They sing together and pray together. They give thanks together and praise together. No discordant note is among them. Why? Verse 21 gives the reason for their harmonious worship: they have an appreciation for and a submission to one another that is born of the Spirit. No one tries to out-do another but rather wants to humble himself before his brother. Their worship together is grounded in their life together.

Praise that Fits

Rejoice in the Lord, O you righteous! For praise from the upright is beautiful.
                                                            Psalm 33:1

Praise and the upright person go together. It is absolutely impossible to think of one apart from the other. The Lord delights in the praises of His people, and there is a distinct beauty, not only in the form of worship and praise, but also in its transforming qualities in the worshiper's life. Praise with thanksgiving and worship from the heart provide a garment visible on the outside and beauty seen on the inside of a person.

The psalmist declares he has been clothed with gladness (Ps. 30:11). In Isaiah 61:3 we are instructed to put on "the garment of praise." Praise is the customary apparel of the upright! If we stop praising, it is as if we are unclothed.

The King James Version of Psalm 33:1 declares "praise is comely for the upright." Maybe it will just make us a little better looking! That is certainly true in our attitudes and relationships. Praisers do not make good complainers. So continue growing as a praising saint. God loves it and it looks good on you!

For the Children

. . . telling to the generation to come the praises of the Lord, and His strength and His wonderful works that He has done.

Psalm 78:4

A key word here is "generation." God's program is large and long; it encompasses all the earth and all time. God has plans that include us and our children.

The interesting thing emphasized here is the continuation of God's program entrusted to the fathers (v. 5). Fathers have the obligation to pass to their children what God has done and said. He commanded our fathers to teach their children. And the fathers are to teach their children even though the fathers themselves have failed in their own commitment to God's way (v. 8). This should say two things to us. First, fathers are not relieved of the responsibility to teach their children even when they have imperfectly followed God's plan. Second, God has not given up hope on His people.

God is concerned about our generation and the next, and the next, and the next. As we praise the Lord for His great works and mighty deeds, we secure for our children the heritage of being God's people.

Desire the Lord

There is none upon earth that I desire besides You. Psalm 73:25

We hear in this verse a cry of complete satisfaction from the psalmist. He has come to the place with God when his heart can say, "Possessing Thee I desire nothing else."

The verses surrounding verse 25 remind us of some facets of this satisfaction. Verse 23 reminds us that God's continual presence with us is a cure for loneliness. In the following verse, there is the provision for guidance, for help when we make decisions. Not many people love to make decisions. What a comfort to know He guides us with His counsel.

In verse 26, His strength is promised for all those times when we realize we cannot go on without Him. Our tomorrows are in His care. He is our portion forever.

Verse 25 sums it all up. It is not what God gives but who He is that satisfies. God is so overwhelmingly important in our lives that all else is of little significance. Let us draw near to God today and get to know Him. Then we can say with the psalmist, "Possessing Thee I desire nothing else."

His Benefits

Bless the Lord, O my soul, and forget not all His benefits.
Psalm 103:2

How do we bless God? God is blessed when we remember and enumerate His benefits. True praise does not have to be worked up; it is the natural consequence of remembering God's benefits to us. Let us look at some of these benefits recorded in this psalm.

I came in with a burden of sin and uncleanness. He cleansed me, and I came out whole (v. 3). Bless God!

I came in crippled with disease and sickness. He released me, healed me, and I came out whole (v. 3). Bless God!

I came in traveling a downward road to the pit, hell, and destruction. He snatched me from it and turned me around, and I came out on the upward way leading to life everlasting (v. 4). Bless God!

He gave me royal standing. I am a child of the King and enjoy the benefits of His kingdom (v. 4). Bless God!

He replaced my dissatisfaction with good things and now my longings are fulfilled (v. 5). Bless God!

Rejoicing

The Lord your God . . . will rejoice over you with gladness.
Zephaniah 3:17

When we are aware of God's great love for us, our hearts respond in worship. To know and receive the gift of His love and acceptance will produce in us an overflow of thanksgiving to Him. When we realize that God actually sings a love song over us and that He sings it loudly with exuberance, our hearts want to respond to Him with song. We are amazed that He delights in us.

The Hebrew words used for "rejoice" and "joy" carry the idea of twirling about with a happy expression on the face, or of a leaping horse romping in the meadow with complete abandon. The Hebrew verb *sus* means "to rejoice, be glad, be greatly happy." From this verb is derived *sason*, a noun meaning "joy, rejoicing, gladness." It describes a rejoicing that is the complete antithesis of mourning; it is a pervasive, irresistible joy.

Let us respond to Him today with a love song. Let us sing and dance before the One who delights in us so completely.

New Beginnings

And the Lord said to Joshua, "This day I will begin to exalt you in the sight of all Israel, that they may know that, as I was with Moses, so I will be with you."   Joshua 3:7

Joshua learned the significance of new beginnings. Moses was gone, but God would use Joshua to make a new beginning.

Nature itself attests to the truth of new beginnings. Each sunrise, each new moon reminds us that God gives us opportunities to begin again. The old day passes with its successes and failures. The former season ends and a new one begins, offering fresh hope. When we tear off the pages from our calendar, we have before us the gift of a new day.

As we praise the Lord of new beginnings, praise Him that He does not banish us to our past, but that His faithfulness to begin again in us is new every morning (Lam. 3:22, 23).

Strength in Praise

Have you never read, "Out of the mouth of babes and nursing infants, You have perfected praise"?   *Matthew 21:16*

*I*n response to the criticism levelled against the powerful praise given Him, Jesus quotes Psalm 8:2 and reminds us of a great secret. Perfected praise will produce strength! It is powerful!

At the very moment when Jesus is being rejected by the religious and political leaders, the praise offered by these young people is more powerful than the present circumstance. While the leaders are attempting to cast doubt on Jesus' authority, the children are captivated by the sudden realization of who Jesus is. Capturing this revelation about Him brings forth loud and powerful praise. And it brings a sudden halt to the proceedings!

Perfected praise will not only operate powerfully in situations; it will produce strength in our own lives. The psalms repeatedly remind us that "The Lord is the strength of my life" (Ps. 27:1; 46:1; 73:26; 118:14). Is there an area where you need strength today? Lift your voice in praise and watch the Lord make you strong in Him!

The Sacrifice of Praise

Let us continually offer the sacrifice of praise to God, that is, the fruit of our lips, giving thanks to His name. Hebrews 13:15

Why is praising God a sacrifice? The word "sacrifice" (Greek, *thusia*) comes from the root *thuo,* a verb meaning "to kill or slaughter for a purpose." Praise often requires that we "kill" our pride, fear, or sloth—anything that threatens to diminish or interfere with our worship of the Lord.

We also discover here the basis of all our praise: the sacrifice of our Lord Jesus Christ. It is by Him, in Him, with Him, to Him, and for Him that we offer our sacrifice of praise to God. Praise will never be hindered when we keep its focus on Him, the Founder and Completer of our salvation.

Paul reminds us to "present your bodies a living sacrifice, holy, acceptable to God, which is your reasonable service" (Rom. 12:1). Jesus' cross, His blood, His love gift of life and forgiveness to us remind us to keep offering continual praise as a living sacrifice before the Lord!

The Armor of Praise

Give them beauty for ashes, the oil of joy for mourning, the garment of praise for the spirit of heaviness. Isaiah 61:3

Praise as a garment is more than a piece of clothing casually thrown over our shoulders. Praise wraps and covers us, leaving no openings through which hostile elements can penetrate. This garment of praise repels and replaces the heavy spirit. This message that Isaiah preached offers instruction and hope for those oppressed by fear or doubt.

In the New Testament, Paul describes another garment that gives this same kind of protective covering (Eph. 6:10–18); he calls it armor. Yet the armor Paul advises us to wear offers us the same advantages: a covering, a protection, and a weapon. He exhorts us to "put on the whole armor of God, that you may be able to stand against the wiles of the devil" (v. 11).

Let us do that today! Allow praise to become your armor. "Put on" this garment. A warm coat from our closet only resists the cold wind when it is "put on." When distressed, be dressed—with praise! Act according to God's Word!

Lovingkindness

*Because Your lovingkindness is better than life, my lips shall
praise You.*   Psalm 63:3

The first five verses of Psalm 63 teach how *expressed*
praise releases the *blessing* of praise. Notice that this
is not a silent prayer: "My mouth shall praise You with joyful lips" (v. 5). And the fruit of this praise is obvious: "God,
You are my God"—affirmed relationship; "early will I seek
You"—clear priorities; "my flesh longs for You"—deep
intensity; "I have looked for You in the sanctuary, to see
Your power and Your glory"—worshiping together with
God's people; "because Your lovingkindness is better than
life, my lips shall praise You"—appropriate gratitude.

This release of praise all begins with a genuine hunger and
thirst for God Himself. Our pursuit of Him delivers to us a
vision of the power of God in the sanctuary, which is just
another dimension of His power in the wilderness. When
we seek Him we find and experience more than just power.
We receive His love. It is His love which makes any life
worth living. So praise Him with joyful lips!

Growing in Praise

I will praise You yet more and more.   Psalm 71:14

The psalmist makes an unwavering commitment. "I will praise You yet more and more." The idea expressed is beautiful: "I will find fresh and new ways to express my praise toward God." The Lord has upheld us from birth (v. 6); He will not abandon us even in our old age (v. 18). As the Lord is willing and able to pour fresh blessing upon us at each turning point in our life, our understanding of His love and power grow. And so must our praise.

This does not mean we must abandon the old ways of praise, but that we are to become as creative in praise to God as God is creative in meeting our needs. If we continue to praise God for the new kindnesses He shows us every day, we will never fall prey to careless or conditioned praise which becomes boring and ends with merely mouthing phrases. The psalmist declares, "My mouth shall tell of . . . Your salvation all the day, for I do not know their limits" (v. 15). So let our praises be hope-filled and unlimited.

Pathway of Praise

Tomorrow's Praise

They may set their hope in God, and not forget the works of God, but keep His commandments.   *Psalm 78:7*

Referring to our children being trained in the way of praise and thanksgiving, the Lord expresses several expectations for them—that they "may not be like their fathers" (v. 8) and that "they may set their hope in God" (v. 7). Children who expect perfect parents will always be disappointed. At some point, fathers will fail. But God still uses fathers to direct children to the unfailing source of hope—God Himself. That generation will succeed that turns its hope away from anything in this life and fastens its hope firmly on God.

In a world set on affixing blame for personal unhappiness and lifelong failure on the circumstances and people of our past, the Lord offers another pathway. As we focus on His faithfulness to our fathers, there is God's unquestionable promise of securing our present and future too. His love for us is real and readily available each day. Learn to praise the Lord for all that He is, for all that He has done, and for a future He has promised to make bright with His presence.

Revival

*Will You not revive us again, that your people may rejoice in
You?*
Psalm 85:6

avid's passion for revival is based upon his desire
that the people rejoice in God. He is not seeking to
rejoice in the blessings of God but in the glory of God's person. He is more desirous of the Giver than of the gift; he is
more desirous of the Father God than the obvious acts of
love and kindness shown him. That is the true essence of
revival.

There were two boys who grew up together on a farm. One
was determined to be rich. He succeeded, becoming a millionaire. The other remained on the farm, married a
woman who loved him, and raised children who loved him
as well. Years later the two met in the Waldorf-Astoria—the
farmer with his wife and two daughters; the millionaire
alone, his wife in Paris, his daughter in London, and his
son on a yacht. He wanted someone to love him, not for
what he had but just for himself. He later died alone of a
broken heart.

God wants us to love *Him,* not for what He gives but for
who He is.

God's Presence

But You are holy, enthroned in the praises of Israel.   Psalm 22:3

Unquestionably, one of the most remarkable and exciting things about honest and sincere praise is taught here: praise will bring the presence of God.

Although God is everywhere present, there is a distinct manifestation of His rule which enters the environment of praise. Here is the remedy for times when you feel alone, deserted, or depressed. Praise! Let this truth create faith and trust, and lead to deliverance from satanic harassments, torment, or bondage. However simply, compose your song and testimony of God's goodness in your life.

The result: God enters! His presence will live (take up residence) in our lives. The Hebrew word translated "inhabit" means "to sit down, to remain, to settle, or marry." In other words, God does not merely visit us when we praise Him, but His presence abides with us and we partner with Him in a growing relationship.

Today, let us invite God's presence into our immediate situation. He wants to come and abide where we are right now!

Deliverance in Praise

*Behold, the wicked brings forth iniquity . . . I will praise the Lord
according to His righteousness.* Psalm 7:14, 17

This short passage contains two vital truths about praise and how we can apply it when we face temptation or the enemy's assault.

First, praise is the answer when wickedness and iniquity come against the believer. Temptation to sin and live wickedly will soon disappear in the face of sincere, powerful, and audible praise. This will not only bring the glorious presence of Jesus, but will drive out the desire to identify with the sinful act or thought. Psalm 18:3 says, "I will call upon the Lord, who is worthy to be praised; so shall I be saved from my enemies." The adversary cannot stand in the face of our praise.

Second, in verse 17 (chap. 7) the writer declares, "I will praise the Lord." Praise is an act of the will. It is not merely an exuberance overflowing with words, but a self-induced declaration of thanksgiving—a sacrifice. The praiser chooses to praise.

No matter what you may face today, offer a thanksgiving of praise to the Lord in the midst of it. It is the best protection you can get!

Pathway of Praise

Knowing the Lord

Enter into His gates with thanksgiving, and into His court with praise. Be thankful to Him and bless his name. Psalm 100:4

Psalm 100 commands us to make a joyful noise, serve the Lord, come into His presence, enter His gates, give thanks to Him, and bless his name. These commands are based on timeless truth: God made us; we are His; we are His people; the Lord is good; His steadfast love endures forever; and His faithfulness is to all generations. Our ability to praise, serve, or enjoy God's presence flows out of our understanding of who God is and who we are in relation to Him.

Everything I am is due to Him. My worship, service, and fellowship with the Creator is dependent upon self-understanding. How can I praise when I am still the center of my own world?

And not knowing the Lord hinders my worship. How can I praise whom I fear? Or bless One whom I think is evil? Or thank One whom I think is capricious? To bless and serve the Lord, I must know Him! Here is the priority: Know the Lord and worship Him with joy!

Lift Up Your Heads

Lift up your heads, O you gates! And be lifted up, you everlasting doors! And the King of glory shall come in. Psalm 24:7

David asks two probing questions in this psalm: "Who may ascend . . . or who may stand in His holy place?" (v. 3), and "Who is this King of glory?" (v. 8). One question asks for the qualifications of the worshiper; the other asks the age-old question, who is the God we worship?

Who stands in His presence? "Those who seek Him" (v. 6). Those with clean hands and pure heart; those who have not lifted up their soul to an idol nor sworn deceitfully. These shall stand. Those who come to God receive blessing and vindication.

Who is the King of glory? He is God the Creator (vv. 1, 2). And the earth is the Lord's. But He is also the personal God of Jacob (vv. 3–6). He is knowable and personally available. He places personal demands on people, and blesses personally and saves personally.

He is God the King, the triumphant God (vv. 7–10). He is strong, mighty in battle, the King of glory! Lift up your heads and the King of glory will come in!

Pathway of Praise

Sing Praises

Sing praise to the Lord, you saints of His, and give thanks at the remembrance of His holy name.   Psalm 30:4

Life is filled with ups and downs. The heights of rejoicing can lead us "into dancing" because of the great things God has done for us. The lows can only be described as "the pit" (v. 9). But God is faithful to His people and gives reason for praise and song.

David declares: "You have lifted me up" and "[You] have not let my foes rejoice over me" (v. 1); "You brought my soul up from the grave" and "You have kept me alive" (v. 3); "[God's] favor is for life" and "joy comes in the morning" (v. 5); and "You have turned for me my mourning into dancing" and "You have put off my sackcloth and clothed me with gladness" (v. 11).

The Lord who loves His people is the One who rescues, delivers, and finishes what we could never do for ourselves. Our praise must come from the depths of our hearts. Therefore, David continues: I must "sing praise to You and not be silent. O Lord my God, I will give thanks to You forever" (v. 12).

Praise Is Beautiful

Praise the Lord! For it is good to sing praises to our God; For it is pleasant, and praise is beautiful.   *Psalm 147:1*

Praise is beautiful! Witness the words of the angel when delivering God's message of salvation to the world, "Glory to God in the highest, and on earth peace, goodwill toward men!" (Luke 2:14). Hear Scripture's testimony of the shepherds, "The shepherds returned, glorifying and praising God for all the things they had heard and seen" (v. 20). They heard the angel and they saw Jesus! After Pentecost the disciples were "praising God" in the midst of the joyous birthing of the church (Acts 2:47). The lame man was healed, and he was "walking, leaping, and praising God" (Acts 3:8). But that is not all.

They praised God in times of distress. Paul and Silas were incarcerated in a Philippian jail. They were taken to court, beaten with many stripes, thrust into the inner prison, feet in stocks—still praising God! Our praise opens the windows of blessing and delights our Father in heaven. "It is good to sing praises . . . it is pleasant, and praise is beautiful."

August

Human Worth

Value of Life

For I have no pleasure in the death of one who dies, says the
Lord God. Therefore turn and live!   Ezekiel 18:32

Life was breathed into man by God. Man was made in the "image" of God and after God's "likeness" (Gen. 1:26; 9:6). Man was God's unique, spiritual, immortal, and intelligent creation. Thus, God commands, "You shall not murder" (Ex. 20:13). To take human life is to assault the image of God in man. Human life should be respected and reverenced. Life, even prenatal life, is always a miracle, and no one should feel he has the right to shed the blood of an innocent human being. In Genesis 9:5, "require" indicates that God was doing more than simply stating a rule. He was saying that He will actually pursue or seek a man's life in payment for the innocent life he has taken.

Where have "world values" begun to shape our minds? Disrespect for human life should not be allowed to invade any mind. Rather, let us proclaim the value and the sacredness of life. Let us take His values as we "turn and live."

Human Worth

One Community

And He has made from one blood every nation of men to dwell on all the face of the earth.   *Acts 17:26*

Here the unity of the human race is clearly stated, for through Adam and Eve (Gen. 3:20), and then through the sons of Noah (Gen. 9:19), all races and nationalities of men came forth. Humankind is a universal family. "Have we not all one Father? Has not one God created us?" (Mal. 2:10). We live in a single world community. No race, nation, or individual has the right to look down on or disassociate itself from another.

The Apostle Peter said, "God has shown me that I should not call any man common or unclean. . . . In truth I perceive that God shows no partiality. But in every nation whoever fears Him and works righteousness is accepted by Him" (Acts 10:28, 34, 35). There are only two divisions of humankind: the saved and the unsaved. Other differences are merely skin deep or culturally flavored.

Today, let us not be guilty of Cain's cry, "Am I my brother's keeper?" The answer to the question is "yes" and it requires our reaching out to the world.

Human Worth

One Body

The body is one and has many members . . . so also is Christ.
1 Corinthians 12:12

The human body is an exquisite organism. Scientists cannot duplicate it or even fully understand it. It is a synthesis of many parts. Each member of the body relates to and depends upon other parts of the body, contributing to the welfare of the entire body.

The same is true of all believers as members of the body of Christ. We should function in Christ's body as the parts of the human body function. Just as the amputation of a limb handicaps the entire body, there is no Christian brother whom we do not need. The Greek word translated "body" is related to the word meaning "to heal, preserve, be made whole." This word clearly shows how our lives are inextricably woven together within the body of Christ and how one's well-being depends upon the well-being of others (Rom. 14:7).

Is there a severed or strained relationship between you and a brother or sister in Christ? Go to him or her today. Allow Christ to knit you together in His Church.

Human Worth

Love One Another

By this all will know that you are My disciples, if you have love for one another.

John 13:35

That Christ would command us to love indicates that love is not just a feeling or a preference; it is how one chooses to relate to others. It is a decision, a commitment, or an action.

Jesus states that the world will know that we are His disciples if we behave lovingly toward one another. Schisms, disputes, unkind criticisms, and defamation of character are contrary to the spirit of Christ. His love is a sacrificial love (John 3:16). It is unconditional love (Rom. 5:8). His love is constant and self-sustaining (Jer. 31:3). His love provides for the best interests of the beloved, and He commands that we should love one another as He has loved us.

Whether that relationship is with a spouse, child, parent, sibling, or friend; and whether that relationship involves failure, hurt, sin, despair, or discouragement, the command remains the same: "love one another." Bring those hurts to Jesus today, and let Him heal and restore your relationships.

Caring Hands

Assuredly, I say to you, inasmuch as you did it to one of the least of these My brethren, you did it to Me.   Matthew 25:40

Throughout Scripture, social consciousness and concern is mandated. The preceding verses to this text specifically tell us Jesus' words on the subject and point out the criterion by which we will be judged: our treatment of those who are hungry, homeless, poor, diseased, and imprisoned (Matt. 25:37–39).

Social concern cannot be divorced from the Christian walk. "If a brother or sister is naked and destitute of daily food . . . but you do not give them the things which are needed for the body, what does it profit? Thus also faith by itself, if it does not have works, is dead" (James 2:15–17). We must not allow the Christian walk to be only a spiritual enterprise, unrelated to our service of humanity. When we fail to care for social need, we fail to place proper value on others, decreasing our own merit in the eyes of the Lord and inviting His condemnation.

Here Jesus equates our treatment of those who are destitute or distressed with our treatment of Himself. What we do for others, we do for Jesus. What will you do for Jesus today?

Human Worth

Love One Another

For I say . . . to everyone who is among you, not to think of himself more highly than he ought to think.   Romans 12:3

Because the Bible teaches that human beings are made in God's image, we are to respect the position of each individual under God. This text does not teach that we believers should think of ourselves as worthless or insignificant beings, but rather that we should give to one another the care each one needs. Possession of different talents or gifts does not denote differences in worth, for all belong to the one body and to one another. Furthermore, all are interdependent (Rom. 12:4, 5).

To think otherwise is to distort reality. When we question the worth of any other part of Christ's body, we are opening ourselves up to the folly of questioning the Most High. While none of us are perfect, the Lord has placed each of us where He wants us, and we can rest in that knowledge (1 Cor. 12:18).

Let us not devalue the ministry and place of one another by thinking of ourselves more highly than we should, but let us live as brothers. Each individual has intrinsic value and worth, and we are all equal before God and in Christ.

Human Worth

Show No Prejudice

But a certain Samaritan, as he journeyed, came where he was.
And when he saw him, he had compassion. Luke 10:33

Jesus lived in a culture filled with prejudice. There was prejudice against the Romans, against the religious leaders, and against women. There was also distinct racial strain between the Jews and Samaritans (John 4:9). They did not frequently interact with one another, and in some cases, outright hostility and hatred existed.

In this parable Jesus used a despised Samaritan to illustrate compassion, which was all the more commendable in that the person the Samaritan assisted, under normal circumstances, probably would not have even spoken to him.

But Jesus consistently brought the life of God to those who were outcast within His culture. We see this as He ministered to the Samaritan woman (John 4:1–26) and the Roman centurion (Luke 7:1–10).

Christ in His coming, has broken down the ultimate barrier of division between us and God (Eph. 2:14). And when we accept His life, He breaks down the barriers between us and one another. Let Him make you free today as He restores trust and relationship.

Human Worth

Abundant Life

The thief does not come except to steal, and to kill, and to destroy. I have come that they may have life, and that they may have it more abundantly. 　　　　　　　　　　　　　*John 10:10*

*C*hrist came to earth in defense of life. By His words and actions He opposed any thing, force, or person that might diminish life. Likewise, He calls us to do everything within our power to preserve and enhance the lives of those around us. Proverbs 31:8 says to "Open your mouth for the speechless, in the cause of all who are appointed to die."

Beyond His defense of life, however, Jesus also came to deliver from death and to introduce abundant living. While He wants us to reach out in ministry, He also wants to fill our lives with purpose and fulfillment. By His death and resurrection, Christ has opened a new dimension of life for all mankind, wherein "all things have become new" (2 Cor. 5:17).

Is there an area of your life where the "thief" has come to steal, kill, or destroy? Turn today to the Lord Jesus who is "able to do exceedingly abundantly above all that we ask or think" (Eph. 3:20).

Human Worth

Salvation

Knowing that you were not redeemed with corruptible things, . . .
but with the precious blood of Christ.   *1 Peter 1:18, 19*

he value of the human being can be inferred from the great price paid to redeem man (John 3:16; 1 Cor. 6:20). God the Son, the Divine One through whom the worlds were created, became flesh and died for the sins of humanity. That He willingly shed His blood and died for us reveals not only the value God places on the human personality, but also shows our desperate need of salvation.

Through Christ, believers are forgiven, reckoned to be righteous, and renewed in the image of God. Fallen men and women can only produce the works of the flesh. Only the Spirit, by the New Birth, can renew and recover that which was destroyed by the Fall (John 3:5, 6).

To reach our highest potential, to have abundant life, to receive forgiveness and be free from condemnation, to live in communion with Father God, and to find renewed purpose for living, we must accept Jesus Christ by faith.

Human Worth

Equal Before Christ

If you show partiality, you commit sin, and are convicted by the law as transgressors.   James 2:9

Human value cannot be equated with race, gender, wealth, social standing, or educational background. All people are significant and valuable in God's order. And He challenges us to place value on all life, however wasted we think that life may be.

The demoniac of Gadara is a case in point (Luke 8:26–39). If there were ever a pointless existence, this appeared to be it. Yet Jesus, in His great compassion, saw worth and purpose in the man's life. He ministered to him, brought him freedom, clothed him, and gave him a purpose.

To regard one race, group, or individual as less important than another is sin, in view of the fact that Christ died for all people and for each one in particular. At the foot of the Cross we are all equal, both in our worth to God (He sent His Son to die for each of us) and in our need to accept His gift of salvation. Let us learn to respect and honor every person and each people. Redemption is for us all.

Human Worth

God Knows

In Your book they all were written, the days fashioned for me, when as yet there were none of them.   Psalm 139:16

I closed my eyes in prayer as the pastor quoted this Scripture over my infant niece at her dedication to the Lord. I so anticipated God's plan for her and how He would hold her hand and guide her through each day of her life.

When she was eight years old, I held her as we wept over her father's untimely death. As I held her, I realized that God's promise was just as real then as it had been at her birth. To this day God had been ahead of both of us, and He already knew our need, our hurt, our anger, and our doubts. He was still there holding our hands.

What a comfort to know that while our future may sometimes look unclear at best, and futile at worst, God knows precisely what lies ahead. The disastrous things that come to us in life are the result of fallen humanity living on a broken planet, but through it all, God's hand is still just as steady and He will lead us.

Human Worth

He Cares for You

[Cast] all your care upon Him, for He cares for you. 1 Peter 5:7

Ephesians 2:14 teaches us that "He Himself is our peace, who has made both one, and has broken down the middle wall of separation." Jesus' death removed the barrier that separated us from the Father; His death now guarantees us the right to cast our cares upon Him.

We often keep our burdens to ourselves because we either do not believe anyone else can or will help, or because we are too ashamed or proud to allow anyone to assist us. But the Lord knows us and our needs, and He still loves us and wants to be our burden-bearer.

It brings great peace to simply know that there is Someone who cares. He cares about you so much that He sent His Son; He broke through all the "red tape" to get to you! He is our peace, and He willingly takes our burdens upon Himself if we will only place them in His hands.

Where are your burdens today? In His hands or yours?

Comfort

May the God of all grace, who called us to His eternal glory by Christ Jesus, perfect, establish, strengthen, and settle you.

1 Peter 5:10

A father who truly loves his child will discipline him (Heb. 12:5, 6) so that the child can become all that he is intended to be. God, as our heavenly Father, is no different; and in the midst of suffering or trial, we are encouraged to see God's gracious hand at work refining and preparing us to be vessels for His glory.

This text tells us that suffering is meant to "perfect, establish, strengthen, and settle [us]." The Greek used here offers insight on what God wants to accomplish through this process. *Katartizo* (perfect) means to complete what is lacking; *sterizo* (establish) points us toward turning resolutely in a certain direction; *sthenoo* (strengthen) means to confirm in spiritual knowledge and power; and *themelioo* (settle) refers to the laying of a foundation.

Be encouraged today! Suffering or trial, in whatever area of life you are experiencing it, will be used to further God's purpose in you. He is making you complete, setting you on His path, filling you with spiritual strength, and laying the foundation of your future.

Human Worth

Purpose—Part 1

I press on, that I may lay hold of that for which Christ Jesus has also laid hold of me.   *Philippians 3:12*

We have not chosen Him but He has chosen us (John 15:16). The Lord has personally selected *you*. Wrapped up in the very word for church is the idea of our being called out. He has called us out of our own plans for our lives, and out of the confusion of our past.

Then once He calls us out, He calls us in, into the excellency of His Kingdom, into communion with Him, and into His plan for our lives.

It may sometimes seem that the plan lies just around the next bend in the road of our spiritual walk with Christ, just beyond our reach or not very well defined. But we "press on" so that we may grasp God's plan for us—the plan that God had in mind when He "grasped" us!

Keep moving on! His plan is there for you! And it is in His plan that you will find your firmest purpose, deepest fulfillment, and highest joy.

Human Worth

Purpose—Part 2

Before I formed you in the womb I knew you; before you were born I sanctified you.

Jeremiah 1:5

God knew us before we were born. He has prenatal perspective on the life He created to serve Him and to bless the world. The Father set us apart with the intent that we would fulfill a distinct purpose in His great plan. Later in this same chapter, the Lord says, "I have put My words in your mouth. . . . I am ready to perform My word" (vv. 9, 12). God does not just call us to serve Him; He also fills us with His Spirit so that the outcome is guaranteed before we even start!

God has created us for Himself, and His plan transcends our lifetime. Revelation 20:6 promises that after Christ's return, we "shall reign with Him a thousand years." We are a precious treasure uniquely created to be an instrument of blessing in the Father's service.

As we go through the day, rest in the knowledge that from before our conception, God's love for us is assured, our purpose has been established, and the power to attain the goal is promised.

Human Worth

Fulfillment

What profit has a man from all his labor in which he toils under the sun?
Ecclesiastes 1:3

The quest of the writer of Ecclesiastes is for a fixed value ("profit") in this life that can serve as a foundation. He examines and discards as bankrupt of real value one item after another. The meaning of life is not to be found in human wisdom, in pleasure, in wealth, in great accomplishments, or in materialism. Even human life itself, in any secular, humanistic sense, cannot be the "profit" which Solomon seeks.

Are we then doomed to despair when we look for meaning in life? No. Underneath his entire quest is the conviction that meaning in life must be found *not* "under the sun," but "above the sun," in the fear and obedience of God (Eccl. 12:13).

As with the Preacher of Ecclesiastes, the challenge to us who live in this age of greed and materialism is not to seek real value in earthly things and comfortable lifestyles, but to concentrate on those things which are above (Col. 3:1). We will find our fulfillment in God alone.

Human Worth

Love Mankind

For there is no distinction between Jew and Greek, for the same Lord over all is rich to all who call upon Him.   Romans 10:12

Paul charges us repeatedly to give all people the same honor. In 1 Timothy 5:21 he adds, "I charge you . . . that you observe these things without prejudice, doing nothing with partiality." And Galatians 2:6 states that God, whom we are to be like, "shows personal favoritism to no man."

That sometimes rankles our human soul. We have our favorites, and we live with the intolerance to which our humanness leads us everyday. Prejudice is ingrained in our sin nature and can be based on anything, from the "wrong" brand of tennis shoes to the "wrong" skin color. And we are warned against simply hiding our prejudices from public view and allowing them to fester in our hearts: "He will surely rebuke you if you secretly show partiality" (Job 13:10). Prejudice has no place in the life of the believer.

Bring prejudices and fears to the Lord today. He wants to purify our souls so that we can "love one another fervently with a pure heart" (1 Pet. 1:22).

Human Worth

Making a Difference

God blessed them, and God said to them, "Be fruitful and multiply; fill the earth and subdue it." Genesis 1:28

Nothing on this earth is more valuable than you! No other form of earthly life plays such a cosmic role as mankind. The world literally stands or falls on the actions of men. Only man has the power to deplete the earth's resources and to pollute its atmosphere. The sin of one man, Adam, corrupted the world (Gen. 6:12, 13).

In contrast, the obedience of one Man, Jesus Christ, brought justification and righteousness to many (Rom. 5:18, 19). If we as His redeemed were to walk perfectly in that justification and righteousness, we could cause the world to bloom and blossom! God wants to reveal His truth and beauty to the world through redeemed mankind.

All of us as believers have strategic significance in our own spheres; we can maximize the impact of the good and encourage others to do the same. We can and will make a difference in our world by the power of the One who lives in us.

Human Worth

Excellence

Then God said, "Let Us make man in Our image, according to Our likeness."   Genesis 1:26

Man is distinct from the rest of creation. God determined that man was to have His "image" and "likeness." Man is a spiritual being. He uniquely contains a soul and spirit. He is a moral being whose intelligence, perception, and self-determination far exceed that of any other earthly being.

These God-given differences possessed by mankind and man's prominence in the order of creation imply his intrinsic worth, not only of the family of mankind, but also of each human individual. The possession of soul and spirit constitutes the essence of what it means to be accountable before God. We should never be pleased to dwell on a level of existence lower than that on which God has made it possible for us to dwell. We should strive for excellence, for our best, for His highest. To do less is to be unfaithful stewards of the life entrusted to us.

Where in your life have you settled for less than God's best? Today He wants to lead you on.

Human Worth

God's Thoughts

For I know the thoughts that I think toward you, says the Lord,
thoughts of peace and not of evil, to give you a future and a
hope.   *Jeremiah 29:11*

In the midst of trial, turmoil, or indecision, we may want to cry out to the Lord as Jesus did on the Cross, "Why have You forsaken me?" We may feel that we are facing the situation alone, but this Scripture gives us tender insight into God's heart toward us. His thoughts toward us are not evil; they are full of expectation, hope, and peace.

The psalmist also wrote about God's thoughts toward us: "The Lord has been mindful of us; He will bless us" (Ps. 115:12). "How precious also are Your thoughts to me, O God! How great is the sum of them! If I should count them, they would be more in number than the sand; when I awake, I am still with You" (Ps. 139:17, 18).

We all face situations where we are tempted to think that God has abandoned us or no longer cares. But rest assured that His thoughts toward us are innumerable, and they are filled with blessing, hope, peace, love, and purpose.

Human Worth

Love the Brethren

And because of your knowledge shall the weak brother perish, for
whom Christ died? 1 Corinthians 8:11

his text refers to the fact that we are to live in a fashion that builds others, rather than in a way that will cause other believers to stumble in their faith. Our responsibility for one another is undeniable and compelling.

First John further asserts that if "someone says, 'I love God,' and hates his brother, he is a liar; for he who does not love his brother whom he has seen, how can he love God whom he has not seen? And this commandment we have from Him: that he who loves God must love his brother also" (1 John 4:20, 21).

The choice of love requires that we hold in tension the two fundamentals of living as brethren: we must live in the liberty of the Lord, and we must live in service to one another. "Do not use liberty as an opportunity for the flesh, but through love serve one another" (Gal. 5:13).

Where is the Lord challenging us to love today? Where is He challenging us to serve?

Human Worth

Made to Rule

You have made [man] a little lower than the angels, and You have crowned him with glory and honor. You have made him to have dominion over the works of Your hands.   Psalm 8:5, 6

Not only is man intrinsically distinct from the rest of creation, but he has been given authority over the earth and everything upon it. Man was made to rule!

While we, as believers in Jesus Christ, often focus our rulership in spiritual realms (Eph. 2:6, 7), mankind's first charge was given for the rulership and well-being of our planet.

The earth's mineral resources, water and air, animal life, and, yes, even the human resources of the earth, all fall under our responsibility and should be the concern of every government and individual. Can we allow to pass from the earth forms of life which the Creator has placed here and committed to our care? Can we risk polluting God's creation? Do we dare to allow needless suffering and the taking of human life? Let there be a resounding "No" in our hearts today as we step into our God-ordained place of rulership.

Human Worth

God Loves Us

I say to you that likewise there will be more joy in heaven over one sinner who repents than over ninety-nine just persons who need no repentance. — Luke 15:7

All of us face that "lost-in-a-crowd" feeling at times. We wonder if anyone notices us, and we are sure no one cares. But the Lord sees us and pursues us with uninhibited love.

To illustrate how much He longs for each of us to know Him, Jesus told a series of parables. He spoke of the shepherd searching for one lost sheep while the ninety-nine were safe in the fold. He told about the woman who swept and cleaned her home until she found the one lost coin. And then, as if telling about inanimate objects or farm animals would not show His heart fully enough, He told the story of the father who lovingly and diligently watched until his lost son returned. "Let's celebrate!" the father cried. "For this my son was dead and is alive again; he was lost and is found" (Luke 15:24).

The next time you are tempted to think no one cares, remember that our Father patiently waits for us and, by the Holy Spirit, lovingly pursues us.

Human Worth

Expect Mighty Things

Call to Me, and I will answer you, and show you great and mighty things, which you do not know.   *Jeremiah 33:3*

We know that if we call on the Lord He will answer. Often, however, our expectations are too small, and we ask based on what we know is possible. But He is the God of the impossible! The Lord sees the situation from every side and has a bigger plan than any of us dream.

He did not choose us to do small things. He chose us to touch people with His love (Lev. 19:34); to see lives changed (Luke 4:18, 19); to raise the next generation of God's people (Deut. 6:7); to exhibit His life in all we do and say (Rom. 8:9, 10); to live as kings and priests of the Most High God (Rev. 1:6); and to rule and reign with Him forever (2 Tim. 2:12; Rev. 22:5).

Let us rejoice today and expect the Lord to do something big through us! For "eye has not seen, nor ear heard, nor have entered into the heart of man the things which God has prepared for those who love Him" (1 Cor. 2:9).

God's Love

But God demonstrates His own love toward us, in that while we were still sinners, Christ died for us.   Romans 5:8

When we were at our worst, God gave us His best. That is comforting to know when we face trial or fall into temptation. God loved us while we were still sinners, and He is not going to give up on us now. "He who has begun a good work in you will complete it" (Phil. 1:6).

The Apostle Paul further reminds us that "God, who is rich in mercy, because of His great love with which He loved us, even when we were dead in trespasses, made us alive together with Christ" (Eph. 2:4, 5). God not only loves us, but He gives us a whole new life! He does not give up on us because He sees all of our potential.

He also calls us to extend that life to those around us. First John 4:11 reminds us that, "If God so loved us, we also ought to love one another." As we rejoice in God's love today, let us extend it to those in need.

Human Worth

Love One Another

Be kindly affectionate to one another with brotherly love, in honor giving preference to one another. Romans 12:10

This Scripture admonishes us to three kinds of love: kindly affection, brotherly love, and giving preference.

"Kindly affection" is drawn from the root word for friend. It implies the cherishing of one's natural relatives. "Brotherly love" suggests that we are to love the brethren—our brothers and sisters in Christ. "Giving preference" requires us to show deference to others. The literal meaning of this word is "to lead the way for others."

Are we doing these things in our lives? Are we living in kindly affection by loving our relatives, honoring our parents, and caring for our families? Are we loving the brethren, or are we constantly criticizing and backbiting? Are we giving preference to those around us? Are we living our lives in such a way that others will come to find Jesus as their Savior and follow Him?

Let us ask the Lord to cause those three areas of love to blossom and grow in our lives as we reach out to our families, the body of Christ, and the world.

Human Worth

We Are Chosen

*You did not choose Me, but I chose you and appointed you that
you should go and bear fruit, and that your fruit should remain.*

John 15:16

At the time of our salvation, the emphasis is on our
making a choice to serve the Lord. We go to the
altar. We repent. We turn to Him. But as in the old adage
that says the girl lets the boy chase her until she catches
him, God had His eye on us long before we turned to Him.
He chose us!

We are sometimes tempted to think we might be that one
person God regretted creating. Or that He was surprised at
our birth. Or that we have such a broken past that there is
no hope for our future. But in God's system of things,
nothing is beyond His gracious plan of redemption! He
loves us with everlasting love (Jer. 31:3), and He drew us to
Himself with gentle cords of love (Hos. 11:4). He chose us.

And He chose us for a purpose. This text says that He has
appointed us to bear fruit and that our fruit should remain.
Let us live in the confidence that God knew what He was
doing when He chose us.

Human Worth

Partnership and Prayer

The effective, fervent prayer of a righteous man avails much.

James 5:16

he Father delights in partnering with us in seeing His will established here on earth. But we recurrently feel at a loss in knowing *how* to be His partner in the task. This text not only provides us with a key to seeing that partnership confirmed, but also with a tangible example of how it can be practically lived out.

The text declares that "Elijah was a man with a nature like ours" (v. 17). He was not any different from you or me. He just stepped into line with the Father's plan and earnestly prayed that His will would be accomplished. Elijah's fervent prayer broke the bonds of drought. Jesus further elaborates, "Whatever you bind on earth will be bound in heaven, and whatever you loose on earth will be loosed in heaven" (Matt. 16:19). Our responsibility is clear: we pray; He releases.

What needs to be changed in your world today? Bring it to the Lord in prayer and then watch Him release the answer in all of His promise and blessing.

God's Love

For God so loved the world that He gave His only begotten Son, that whoever believes in Him should not perish but have everlasting life.　　　　　　　　　　　　　　　　　　　　*John 3:16*

We cannot begin to fathom the great sacrifice God made for us in sending His Son or to consider such selfless love. The word used here for "love" is *agapao*. We more often recognize it as *agape,* and it is a uniquely Christian word. In the time of the New Testament it was virtually unused by writers outside of the believing community.

Agapao is the word used for God's unconditional love. It is love by choice. It does not need a "chemistry," an affinity, or a feeling. The word denotes unconquerable benevolence and undefeatable goodwill. *Agapao* will never seek anything but the highest good for mankind.

God, in His infinite, unconditional love for us, knew that the highest good for mankind would require the death of His Son—the ultimate sacrifice that can be made by a father. Yet, the Father and the Son willingly made that sacrifice because of Their great love for us.

As we live in the life of God's love, let us also live in constant praise for Jesus' death for us and the Father's gift to us.

Human Worth

Love One Another

Love does no harm to a neighbor; therefore love is the fulfillment of the law.   *Romans 13:10*

This text indicates that when we show love for one another, we automatically fulfill the law, and if we truly love, we will not do anything that is harmful to others. We will keep everything in right priority and become sensitive to the needs of others.

First Corinthians 13 is called the love chapter, and it gives us a clear definition on how love is to conduct itself: "Love suffers long and is kind; love does not envy; love does not parade itself, is not puffed up; does not behave rudely, does not seek its own, is not provoked, thinks no evil; does not rejoice in iniquity, but rejoices in the truth; bears all things, believes all things, hopes all things, endures all things. Love never fails" (1 Cor. 13:4–8).

Let us reach to the people around us with God's law of love that brings healing, comfort, and joy.

Human Worth

We Are Royalty

Behold what manner of love the Father has bestowed on us, that we should be called children of God!   1 John 3:1

Our culture tells us that there is no one so special that he cannot be replaced. But God created each of us unique, and we are so loved, that the King of kings has chosen to adopt us and to call us His own children. That makes us royalty!

Royalty in our world enjoys incredible wealth, mingles with the "jet set," and has worldwide fame. But they also face their inability to change the world situation and have to deal with scandal, gossip, and lack of privacy. They cannot call their lives their own.

And neither can we. Scripture says that we were bought with a price (1 Cor. 7:23) and that now we belong to Father God. We are part of a more worthy royal line: The Father has made us His noble and virtuous children (Ps. 45:13). We follow the law of another kingdom (James 2:8). We are now fulfilling a new call on our lives (1 Pet. 2:9).

Let us conduct ourselves today as befits a child of the King.

Human Worth

September

Spiritual Warfare

Jesus' Prayer

Satan has asked for you, that he may sift you as wheat. But I have prayed for you, that your faith should not fail.
Luke 22:31, 32

The eternal struggle is lived out everyday in our hearts, families, and places of service. There is no surprise in our being opposed by the adversary. Never are the words of our Savior more welcome, "I have prayed for you."

The heavenly Intercessor, our Creator and Redeemer, declares that He has seen the plan of the adversary for our demise, and He is mounting a counterassault in our behalf to break the power of the enemy. Having vanquished the devil at Calvary, Jesus welcomes the opportunity to defeat him again in the battleground of our lives. Despite the temporary incursions into our character, where compromise can creep in almost unnoticed; in our relationships, which bear the bruises of not just human misunderstanding but outright demonic attack; and in our sin, driven by pride and fear, still our faith in Christ will not fail.

Jesus understands the nature of our condition and the ferocity of the contest. He alone stands as the ever-ready guarantor of our life and future in Him.

Spiritual Warfare

Eyes of Faith

*Do not fear, for those who are with us are more than those who
are with them.*   *2 Kings 6:16*

At this moment Elisha and his servant are surround-
ed by the great Syrian army. In Israel's war with
Syria, Elisha's prophetic insight has continually given away
Syrian battle strategies. The army is here attempting to end
Israel's prophetic advantage.

Prayer is the vital turning point in this entire passage. First,
it is through prayer that the strategies of the adversary are
discerned. Second, prayer is the key to dispelling the panic
of Elisha's servant. After declaring that the Syrians are outnumbered by the two of them, Elisha prays. He does not
pray that the Lord will show his servant yet another miracle; he asks that he be able to see into another dimension.

The answer came immediately. "And behold, the mountain
was full of horses and chariots of fire all around Elisha" (v.
17). They had always been there. The Lord had anticipated their need and provided. However, it was only through
eyes of faith in the spiritual realm that the resource could
be seen. So today, don't be afraid! Look up with eyes of
faith. The Lord has outnumbered your enemies!

Spiritual Warfare

Worship—Part 1

Now when they began to sing and to praise, the Lord set ambushes against the people of Ammon, Moab, and Mount Seir, . . . and they were defeated.   2 Chronicles 20:22

*I*n this text, Judah is about to be overwhelmed by a confederation of three opposing armies. Its armies are hopelessly outnumbered and face certain defeat, but God has a plan—Worship!

Worship puts God in His proper place as Creator of the universe, Redeemer of our life, and Provider of everything we need. Because we know whom we worship, our worship releases the Lord to perform His purpose within us. Worship is not blissful ignorance or vain superstition in the face of present need. It is confirming God's desire to work in the lives of His people.

Spiritual power is released through praise! Here the enemies of Judah (literally "praise" in Hebrew) are confused and begin to slaughter each other as the people of God begin to sing and worship. Jehoshaphat, Judah's king, never sends the army to fight, only the choir! In the same way, the Lord promises that as we face each challenge with praise, He will confuse and scatter the enemy.

Whatever today may bring, no matter how large the obstacle, the beginning point of breakthrough is worship.

Spiritual Warfare

Worship—Part 2

"As Commander of the army of the Lord I have now come." And Joshua fell on his face to the earth and worshiped. Joshua 5:14

Having just crossed the Jordan, and with the promised land now under his feet, Joshua and the people of Israel began the process of possessing the promise which began a generation before when the Lord led Israel out of Egyptian bondage. The Lord Himself now stands before Joshua, outfitted for combat, ready to lead Israel into battle. It was clear there would be no conquest without battle; yet, the scene is familiar.

A generation earlier Moses stood before Sinai's burning bush, and the Lord spoke to him, calling him to lead Israel out of bondage. He, like Joshua now, was instructed to "take off your shoes." The Commander's assignment had to begin with worship.

Standing on man-made plans, human strength, or fleshly desire will never accomplish deliverance from sin's bondage or the possession of God's promise for our lives. Our bare-footed, empty-handed, fall-on-your-face-before-the-Lord dependence is the one sure route to ultimate freedom in our personal lives and victory for those we lead.

Repentance

You cannot stand before your enemies until you take away the accursed thing from among you.   Joshua 7:13

Achan's lust for treasure had brought disaster to Israel's pursuit in possessing the land of promise. Therefore, the Lord said, "You cannot stand before your enemies." Here, the sin of one man temporarily brought a halt to the progress of an entire nation. The hideous power of sin to corrupt God's people and to stall His purpose among them is clearly illustrated in this passage.

Yet, Romans 5:17 triumphantly reminds us, "For if by the one man's offense death reigned through the one, much more those who receive abundance of grace and of the gift of righteousness will reign in life through the One, Jesus Christ." The power of one man's sin—Adam's, Achan's, yours, or mine—is completely broken through the righteousness of God's only Son.

Whenever we feel disqualified or disabled through sin, there is grace for those who repent, forgiveness for those who respond in faith, and a future of redeemed promise for those who will humble themselves to receive it.

Spiritual Warfare

Obedience

[They] blew the trumpets and broke the pitchers—they held the torches . . . they cried, "The sword of the Lord and of Gideon!"

Judges 7:20

Israel's enemy is routed by thirty pot-breaking, torch-carrying, ear-splitting warriors who never shoot an arrow, throw a spear, or wield a sword. Here, simple obedience to God's directives brings liberation to God's people. The spiritual conflict was not won on human terms in the sweaty, close quarters of combat, or in human force with a numberless host trained and hardened for battle. It was decided on the basis of faithful response to the things the Lord had spoken to Gideon.

Human nature demands that we stack things in our favor, gathering every possible human resource to confront our challenges. And, all along, the Holy Spirit continually reminds us that our sufficiency is in Him alone.

Our resources for success in life have little to do with what we can arrange, and everything to do with what we invite the Lord to work in us and through us by His grace. All He requires is that we be faithful to His commands.

Prayer

Call to Me, and I will answer you, and show you great and mighty things.
                                        Jeremiah 33:3

What an absolutely incredible promise! If Jeremiah prays, God promises that He will not only answer him, but reveal "great and mighty things." These are things that could not possibly be known any other way. The idea of the word "mighty" in Hebrew would be better rendered "isolated" or "inaccessible." God is offering revelational insight based upon a pursuit of Him in prayer.

All successful, spiritual enterprise is based upon clear understanding of the forces which oppose us and direction for dealing with these influences. The carnal mind is unfit for spiritual warfare. Our natural human perception can at best only lead us to the doorway of understanding and never through it. Even former spiritual victories and the experience of walking with Christ for years cannot substitute for fresh spiritual insight that comes from our daily walk with Him in prayer.

How is your prayer life today? Turn to the Lord now and He will provide all that we need: guidance, insight, strength . . . and "great and mighty things."

Spiritual Warfare

Trust

Trust in the Lord with all your heart and lean not on your own understanding; in all your ways acknowledge Him, and He shall direct your paths.   *Proverbs 3:5, 6*

*W*e cannot trust someone we do not know. These verses hold two key words to discovering a loving, trustworthy Lord at work in our personal lives.

We are to acknowledge the Lord in all our ways. The word used here for "ways," Hebrew *derek,* means "a road, a course, or a mode of action." It suggests specific opportunities a person may encounter on a regular basis. Seeing His hand at work in the everyday places opens our heart to trust in times of deepest trial.

Then, "acknowledge," Hebrew *yada,* means "to know by observation, investigation, or firsthand experience." The highest level of knowledge is direct intimate contact. This refers to the life-giving intimacy of marriage. Applied to our spiritual lives, it suggests that prayer conceives and gives birth to blessings and victories.

As seen in the light of this text, we may conclude that if in all our days we maintain contact with God, He promises to direct our paths toward fruitful, life-begetting endeavors.

Prayer—Part 1

My voice You shall hear in the morning, O Lord; in the morning I will direct it to You, and I will look up.   Psalm 5:3

Consistent, daily prayer, or "morning by morning," as verse 3 can be translated, is a beginning point to spiritual effectiveness in prayer. David uses the Hebrew word *'arak* "direct," in the declaration that he would direct his petitions to God daily. *'Arak* is most frequently used in Moses' writings in reference to the priests "setting in order" the sacrifices to be brought before the Lord each day (Ex. 40:4). It also describes an army being "set in array" in preparation for battle (Judg. 20:20–22). This indicates an ordered strategy for battle. Thus, David declares here that he had a well-thought-out order to his prayers, a daily prayer strategy filled with purpose and meaning.

What a joy to bring before the Lord everyday a new sacrifice of our lives (Rom. 12:1), and to prepare ourselves systematically for spiritual warfare. Our greatest victories are rarely won in an instant, but in the morning-by-morning application of His truth and power which overthrows the strongholds of darkness in our world and secures His purpose in us.

Prayer—Part 2

The effective, fervent prayer of a righteous man avails much.
James 5:16

Energeo—it takes two English words to translate it: effective, fervent. The Apostle Paul used this same word in describing the power of God's Word in our lives: "You welcomed it not as the word of men, but as it is in truth, the word of God, which also effectively works in you who believe" (1 Thess. 2:13). God's work in us grows because the force of this new life is Holy Spirit power, and it keeps changing us into the image of our Savior, Jesus Christ. *Energeo* describes a process that is far more than energetic; *energeo* accomplishes its goal.

The fervency of the prayer described in this verse is not based in pointless emotionalism. It is a passion in prayer that is confident of certain fulfillment. It is based upon the surety of God's partnership in bringing His kingdom rule into our world as we pray.

As we pray today, let us pray believing. The Holy Spirit provides the *energeo* that continues until the righteous purpose of God has prevailed. Our prayers work!

Intercession

*So I sought for a man among them who would make a wall, and
stand in the gap before Me . . . but I found no one.*

Ezekiel 22:30

*J*ust one person would have made the difference! God
sought that person. How many situations are there
today, in our world, where the Lord is looking for just one
person to stem the tide of sin's hideous destruction? He is
not looking for a perfect person, just one who will stand
before Him on behalf of the people who cannot stand for
themselves.

The devil would make cowards of us all, should we have to
stand before the prince of evil all alone. But the invitation
to the intercessor is to stand before the throne of all grace
and love, with Jesus at the right hand of the Father. There
we plead our case as intercessors.

The Son of God (the final Advocate for us all) confirms our
intercession and the power of God is released to flow to the
places where devastation is in process and God's redemption is now welcomed. And it only takes one. Let us learn
to steward our privilege with sensitivity and to respond as
He seeks us out to be the one who stands in the gap.

Spiritual Warfare

A Mighty Fortress

Put on the whole armor of God, that you may be able to stand against the wiles of the devil.   *Ephesians 6:11*

Spiritual warfare? The darkness of the demonic? The gifts of the Spirit? All new themes in the church today? Read on:

A mighty fortress is our God, a bulwark never failing; Our helper He, amid the flood of mortal ills prevailing. For still our ancient foe doth seek to work us woe; his craft and pow'r are great, and, armed with cruel hate, on earth is not his equal.

Did we in our own strength confide, Our striving would be losing; were not the right Man on our side, The Man of God's own choosing. Dost ask who that may be? Christ Jesus, it is He; Lord Sabaoth, His name, from age to age the same, and He must win the battle.

That word above all earthly pow'rs, no thanks to them, abideth; the Spirit and the gifts are ours thro' Him who with us sideth. Let goods and kindred go, this mortal life also; the body they may kill. God's truth abideth still, His kingdom is forever. Amen.

To Martin Luther's words from four and a half centuries ago, say "Amen!"

Spiritual Warfare

Holy Spirit Release

They were all filled with the Holy Spirit, and they spoke the word of God with boldness.

Acts 4:31

The Greek word for boldness, *parhesia*, means "outspoken, unreserved utterance, freedom of speech, frankness, candor, cheerful courage, the opposite of cowardice." Here, it is divine enablement that comes to ordinary people exhibiting spiritual power and authority. *Parhesia* is not a human quality, but a result of being filled with the Holy Spirit.

Earlier in verse 29, the believers prayed, "Lord . . . grant to Your servants that with all boldness they may speak Your word." Be careful what you pray for, because that is what you are going to get! As they prayed the place was shaken, and they were all filled with the Holy Spirit. They spoke with *parhesia*.

Today there are people waiting for you to speak boldly, not the words of human comfort, but the powerful words of God that will set them free. Bound by sin, confused by meaningless lives, hopeless and unloved, the world around us cries out for someone to help. Let us boldly proclaim Jesus and demonstrate His all-powerful and all-loving concern for them.

Spiritual Warfare

Holy Spirit Release

Now the multitude of those who believed were of one heart and one soul.   Acts 4:32

The release of true Holy Spirit power is directly relat- ed to the unity of the believers. Jesus prayed for unity in John 17, and He instructs us in Matthew 18:19 that the prayer of agreement knows no limit to its ability to release God's power. And here in Acts, unity is the direct result of the Holy Spirit's filling—"those who believed were of one heart and one soul."

Human pride is the culprit that divides brothers and sisters in the Body of Christ. It is the foremost device of the adversary to thwart the flow of God's power by bringing reproach to the Church in a watching world.

Pride has the same devastating effect in homes. Marriages are broken and children are lost because loveless pride divides families. True Holy Spirit power melts hearts and brings us to unity in soul. While it does not guarantee a universality of thought, we do become melted in love and in His unlimited power move together with one heart.

Holy Spirit Release

And with great power the apostles gave witness to the resurrection of the Lord Jesus. And great grace was upon them all. Acts 4:33

The gathering shook with the power of God, but the intention was to shake loose the city. Charged with supernatural power, the apostles preach the Gospel and confront the spiritual forces which hold the city in darkness and fear. Though bullied by jailing, and threatened by the same power structure that crucified Jesus, they are continually being filled with the Holy Spirit. The revival that began at Pentecost, continuing in miracle signs and wonders, now reduces the forces of darkness to empty threats before the genuine power of the living Church in action.

The lying threats of the devil are no match for the unmistakable power of the Holy Spirit. Demons would intimidate us into silence, torment us with fears, and bring despair through circumstance unless we, as Spirit-filled believers in Christ, receive a fresh work of Holy Spirit power each day. Ask for this power. Be renewed for today's challenge and let the power of Jesus Christ bring "great grace" upon each of us right now.

Spiritual Warfare

Our Defense

For the accuser of our brethren, who accused them before our God day and night, has been cast down.   Revelation 12:10

The devil is a liar. But that is not all. He is a defeated liar! Though he accuses us before God for our weakness and our sin, Jesus' answer on our behalf is dramatic and instant, "Father, forgive them." Denied in heaven, the work of the accuser seeks to find a hearing among the fleshy ears of those who are vulnerable to criticize brothers and sisters in the Body of Christ. Or his words burn in the minds of those condemned by the failure of their own lives.

But rejoice, beloved. "There is therefore now no condemnation to those who are in Christ Jesus" (Rom. 8:1). The accuser has been cast down. Confess sin and be healed, but reject the lying words of a defeated foe. Our debt has been paid, our ransom complete, our shame covered by the grace of God. Rejoice, the One who saves us is the same One who accepts us, and by the work of His Holy Spirit continues the process of His renewing work in us.

Spiritual Warfare

Faith

So Jesus answered and said to them, "Have faith in God."
Mark 11:22

These words of our Lord follow the Savior's cursing the fig tree, indicating a passion in prayer and faith that we need to learn. When the disciples later noticed with surprise that the tree had withered (v. 20), Jesus responded with a sharp command, "Have faith in God." Then, calling His followers to "speak to the mountains," He led them to prepare for situations in which they would find it necessary to take direct authority in the spiritual realm to impact things in the natural realm.

The issue of faith is never founded on our ability to "move the mountain," but faith in the Mountain-maker. Visualizing a victory or working up a "feeling" of faith is a pathetic human attempt to get something to happen. Real faith lays hold of the Faith-giver (Eph. 2:8), who holds all power for every need, and trusts Him to answer our prayer as He promised He would do.

As faith-challenging situations arise, turn to the Lord. He is waiting for you to call upon Him.

Spiritual Warfare

Passion for God's Presence

And you will seek Me and find Me, when you search for Me with all your heart.
                                                    Jeremiah 29:13

The Lord promises His people "a future and a hope" earlier in this passage. But this promise is based on a passion for His presence. The word "search" suggests an earnestness that borders on desperation, a close pursuit of God with diligence.

The passionate pursuit of anything seems foreign to our modern culture that cloaks itself in a carefree nonchalance. But God's Word shows us the desire of His people to seek Him. Psalm 84:2 declares, "My soul longs, yes, even faints for the courts of the Lord; my heart and my flesh cry out for the living God." There is no discovery of the Lord and His delivering power for those who do not passionately pursue it.

The pressure of a sinful world and the unrelenting yearning of our flesh deny entry into the courts of the Lord to those who carelessly attempt to saunter in. But for those whose hearts are aflame, there can be no force of flesh or devil that can prevent our finding the Lord's grace, bringing us "a future and a hope."

Spiritual Warfare

Fasting

Then I proclaimed a fast there at the river of Ahava, that we might humble ourselves before our God.   Ezra 8:21

The power of the fast is found in the abject humility of people who desire the Lord's way in their lives more than the bread that sustains their physical bodies. Fasting is an announcement the soul makes that the body will not rule over it, and it declares there will be no relief until the issues set before God are resolved in spirit. Fasting does not signal sincerity but rather humbles the soul with dependence upon God.

During his fast Ezra sought the Lord for direction for the families with him and for protection of both the people and the possessions God had given them. Isaiah 58:6 focuses the fast on loosing "bonds of wickedness," undoing "heavy burdens," and freeing "the oppressed." The hunger and discomfort of the fast are reminders to pray, be in the Word, and demonstrate the living Word of our Savior, that "man shall not live by bread alone, but by every word that proceeds from the mouth of God" (Matt. 4:4).

Answering God's Call

When you go to war . . . you shall sound an alarm with the trumpets . . . and you will be saved from your enemies. Numbers 10:9

*T*he Lord's instruction to Moses was clear, "make two silver trumpets." One trumpet was to call the people to gather, the other to move forward, usually sounding the advance into battle. "You shall sound an alarm with the trumpets . . . and you will be saved from your enemies."

A people alerted to danger and aligned for battle are a formidable obstacle for any invading force. Paul warns that without a trumpet warning disaster is certain. "For if the trumpet makes an uncertain sound, who will prepare for battle?" (1 Cor. 14:8). As God's people hear the sounding of the trumpet of the Holy Spirit's call to spiritual warfare, they prepare for the works of darkness. Moving in unity and prayer, they resist the attack of the devil.

The Bible describes another trumpet in Revelation 11:15. This is the last trumpet, announcing once and for all that "the kingdoms of this world have become the kingdoms of our Lord and of His Christ, and He shall reign forever and ever!" Maranatha, Lord, come quickly. We wait to hear that last trumpet call of all.

Spiritual Armor—Part 1

Put on the whole armor of God, that you may be able to stand against the wiles of the devil.   Ephesians 6:11

*I*t is unthinkable! No one would do it! No one in his right mind would leave the house for the day naked. Not only does it break social convention, but it leaves you unprotected from the elements.

Every day, however, Christians leave their homes unprotected from the spiritual elements they will face. And as surely as we are naked without our clothes, we are just as naked for spiritual combat without our armor. The armor of God is something we put on and keep on, because every day is a day of spiritual conflict. The unprotected are victimized or wounded.

The assault of the devil is unrelenting, cunning, and constantly searching for any place in our defenses that is uncovered. Whether to cause us to doubt God's love for us, or compromise our integrity, or confuse us with doctrines of lies and half truths, our only defense is to dress for battle every day. Girded with truth, covered by righteousness, shielded by faith, and transformed by salvation, we are ready to face the day.

Spiritual Warfare

Spiritual Armor—Part 2

[Take] the shield of faith . . . quench all the fiery darts of the wicked one. And take the helmet of salvation, and the sword of the Spirit, which is the word of God.   *Ephesians 6:16, 17*

Spiritual warfare demands supernatural implements for victory in battle. Paul describes three vital pieces of equipment: the shield of faith, the helmet of salvation, and the sword of the Spirit. Our faith in the nature of our God and His sovereign ability to keep us from harm and protect us from the vicious onslaught of the enemy offers a shield of coverage no enemy arrow can penetrate. The helmet of salvation provides a transformation of our thinking and power to live for Jesus under the devil's duress (Rom. 12:2). The sword of the Spirit offers us a weapon that never grows dull and never becomes too heavy for us to handle, even in times of weariness and discouragement.

Step out today, though our adversary would lie, threaten, frighten, and seek to disable us. God's Word is sure; His sword will not fail you. Our faith is strong. Centered in Him, it offers all the protection we will ever need. And the Lord has supplied us with the strategy and ability to act upon His purpose for us, until our enemies are defeated and His promise is secured.

Ministry of Tears

Those who sow in tears shall reap in joy. He who continually goes forth weeping, bearing seed for sowing, shall doubtless come again with rejoicing, bringing his sheaves with him.

Psalm 126:5, 6

Tears play a unique role in spiritual breakthrough. This text tells us that the planting of seeds accompanied by a spirit of brokenness will not only bring a spiritual harvest of results, but will leave the sower with a spirit of rejoicing in the process. Scripture teaches us that tears have a variety of purposes and functions related to what might be termed "the ministry of tears."

Tears of sorrow (2 Kin. 20:5) are brought on by the helplessness of our physical frailty. Tears of joy (Gen. 33:4) rejoice in relationships restored. There are tears of compassion (John 11:35) in caring for the pain of others. Then there are tears of desperation (Esth. 4:1, 3), crying out for the help only God can give. We weep tears of travail (Is. 42:14) in bearing down to give birth to the new thing God has promised to do. There are tears of repentance (Joel 2:12, 13), weeping because of our sin.

It is in our heart, softened by tears, where we must plant. And in such fertile soil, the precious seeds will grow and bring a joyous and abundant harvest.

Spiritual Warfare

The Real Enemy

For we do not wrestle against flesh and blood, but . . . against
spiritual hosts of wickedness in the heavenly places.

Ephesians 6:12

The target is clearly defined; our enemy is spiritual. Keeping a clear focus on the true nature of our demonic assailants is essential. So much of a believer's time is wasted, energy expended, and injury incurred because we spend ourselves battling people (flesh and blood) instead of the spiritual forces at work in a situation. In the process of attempting to wrestle believers into defeat in their personal lives, the devil attempts to divert the force of our "spiritual" warfare toward others—in our families, our churches, our work place and community.

The devil knows full well these two things: (1) if we start fighting other people, they will certainly oblige us and fight back, and (2) that if we start fighting each other, we will never get around to defeating him.

So, whatever (or whoever) you face today, make up your mind about the conflict. Our enemy is the devil. As we make war in prayer and make peace with those around us, the devil stands no chance of succeeding in our lives.

Spiritual Warfare

Spiritual Authority

Behold, I give you the authority to trample on serpents and scorpions, and over all the power of the enemy, and nothing shall by any means hurt you.   Luke 10:19

Our authority is His. When Jesus gave the disciples *exousia*, He gave them delegated authority, the right to act, ability, and capacity. Since Jesus had the *exousia* to forgive sins, heal sicknesses, and cast out devils, what He passed along to His disciples was the power to function as He did. Jesus gave His followers this *exousia*, and it has never been rescinded (John 14:12). And because He has delegated to us this privilege, it is now our responsibility to exercise it in His name.

The issue is certainly not to stomp on snakes and huge bugs, but to face the most fearsome works of hell and see them overcome in the power of God's Spirit. As we use the power He has given us, "nothing shall by any means hurt you." How much pain do we suffer because in fear or neglect we surrender this privilege to operate with such authority. The serpent will bite; the scorpion will sting; the enemy will attack. But as we use the *exousia* He has given us, we will overcome the works of darkness.

Spiritual Warfare

Spiritual Authority

Nevertheless do not rejoice in this, that the spirits are subject to you, but rather rejoice because your names are written in heaven.

Luke 10:20

Man's fascination with the supernatural is well recorded throughout all of history. Here Jesus addresses His own disciples' preoccupation with their triumph over demonic forces. Neither dismissing its significance nor diminishing their joy, Jesus is helping them identify true priorities for the people of faith.

First, it should be of no surprise that demons were cast out by the disciples. Jesus gave them His power. This power is essential for living as spiritual people in a demon-filled world. But it is not for show or to "prove" their power.

Second, the single-most treasured truth and demonstration of divine power is the Lord's love, forgiveness, and eternity in exchange for our weakness, sin, and humanity. There is no greater power than that which saves a sinner from hell. There is no comparison to be made. Casting out demons is accomplished in Jesus' authority; however, the rescue of a sinner required the sacrifice of His life.

Let us set our priorities to move in the power of His Spirit and live in the fullness of His saving grace.

Spiritual Warfare

Prayer

For the weapons of our warfare are not carnal but mighty in God for pulling down strongholds.   *2 Corinthians 10:4*

We are citizens of two worlds. We are spiritual people redeemed by the Lord to live as His people in the kingdom of God; and, simultaneously, we are human beings living in a very physical world still plagued by the nature of our father, Adam. But our warfare is spiritual. It may look physical, evoking strong emotion with obvious fleshly targets, but the Apostle Paul declares that our battle is spiritual and the only true effective implements for our warfare are spiritual, too.

These implements are "mighty" because they are spiritual, attacking the source of the problem. Satanic strongholds resist the advance of God's kingdom, and devilish arguments boast themselves against God. These opponents will not yield to human reason, earthly passion, or man-made device.

Prayer translates spiritual action into practical breakthrough. Our warfare demands Spirit-filled, Bible-quoting, Holy Ghost-directed, supernatural prayer. This prayer casts down the works of the devil, shuts the mouth of the liar, and restores the minds of those captured by their own disobedience.

Spiritual Warfare

Unity

Every kingdom divided against itself is brought to desolation, and a house divided against a house falls.   Luke 11:17

Paul asks the church in Corinth the searching question, "Is Christ divided?" (1 Cor. 1:13). Sadly, in the first-century church, each one had his own faction, each one was right in his own eyes, each sensed his own unique destiny in the Lord. Well, here it is. The challenges we face today are no different. The adversary still attempts to strip the power of the Body of Christ by separating believers.

It is our love for the Lord and His love in us for brothers and sisters in the Body of Christ that create an unshakable house. The differences of tradition, style, and ministry focus reflect our uniquenesses in Christ. Our love, acceptance, and encouragement for others in the Body of Christ is the verification of His love at work in us. Let us daily allow the love of God to grow our hearts bigger, making room for the family of God to grow ever stronger.

Love Casts Out Fear

There is no fear in love; but perfect love casts out fear. . . . But he who fears has not been made perfect in love.   *1 John 4:18*

Christianity gave love (Greek *agape*) a new meaning. This word rarely occurs in existing non-biblical Greek manuscripts of the period. *Agape* denotes an undefeatable benevolence and unconquerable goodwill that always seeks the highest good of the other person, no matter what he does. It is the selfless love that gives freely, without asking anything in return, and does not consider the worth of its object. *Agape* is a love by choice, and it refers to the will to love rather than the emotion of love. *Agape* describes the unconditional love God has for the world.

His love for the world and toward each of us is complete. Fear grips our souls because we are more convinced of the triumph of circumstance and sin over us than the undefeatable unconquerable love that securely holds us. We are His and He finds us precious.

Today He will keep us, love us, and if we will hold tightly to Him, He will drive our fears far from us.

The Cross

*My preaching [was] not with persuasive words of human wisdom
. . . that your faith should not be in the wisdom of men but in the
power of God.*　　　　　　　　　　　　　*1 Corinthians 2:4, 5*

The Apostle Paul's greatest concern in ministry was
that he should preach nothing but Christ and His
cross. He did not preach to show off his oratorical skills;
rather, he spoke with "fear, and . . . trembling," denoting
the opposite of self-confidence. "In the power of God" not
only refers to the miracles that accompanied Paul's preaching (2 Cor. 12:12), but also to the Holy Spirit's transforming power in the individual lives of the Corinthians when
they were converted. Far from a mere intellectual conver-
sion through human wisdom, they encountered the Spirit
Himself who demonstrated His miraculous presence in
them.

The cross of Jesus Christ is the power of God. It is a point
of ridicule for those who are perishing in their sins, but it
is the only power to save for those who believe. All of life's
final issues are settled at the cross: human pride vs. God's
provision, man's sin vs. God's love, our adversary the devil
vs. God's perfect Son. Here at the cross Jesus cried, "It is
finished."

Let the power of this finished work happen in you today.

Spiritual Warfare

October

Reaching the World

Universal Blessing

*I will make you a great nation; I will bless you . . . and in you
all the families of the earth shall be blessed.* *Genesis 12:2, 3*

God's promise to Abraham was blessing. God blessed
him with wealth, honor, and offspring to whom He
gave the "promised land" of Canaan. But as great as such
blessings were, God's greatest blessing to Abraham was His
everlasting covenant or pledge "to be God to you and your
descendants after you" (Gen. 17:7). In contrast to wealth,
honor, offspring and a land, this blessing could be passed
on to "all the families of the earth." God chose Abraham
from idolatrous Ur so Abraham could both know Him *and*
make Him known.

God's specific promise to Abraham had a universal purpose: "I will bless you that you might be a blessing . . . to all
nations." In Christ Jesus a personal relationship with God
through the gift of the Spirit is available for all people. The
good news of Jesus Christ is not only to be believed and
enjoyed; it also is to be shared and passed on to "all
nations." Have you received the good news? Are you passing it on?

Reaching the World

A Priestly Kingdom

You shall be to Me a kingdom of priests and a holy nation.

Exodus 19:6

God promised to bless Abraham and make him a blessing to all nations. He repeated this promise to his son, Isaac (Gen. 26:5, 6) and to his grandson, Jacob (Gen. 28:12–14), as well. God chose Abraham and his descendants so they could not only know Him, but also make Him known. Years later God sent Moses to demand of Pharaoh, "Let my people go!" But why? "That they might worship Me!" (Ex. 4:23). Their worship of the one true God was to be a witness to all nations of God's power to save.

This world is under the rule of an alien king, the god of this age, the devil. But God's redemptive mission has begun. King Jesus has come to set His people free to live to the praise of God's glory. His liberated people are His "special treasure." As His loyal subjects they are a "kingdom of priests" with the priestly duty of proclaiming the gospel of God, so that the nations might become an offering acceptable to God, sanctified by the Holy Spirit (Rom. 15:16).

House of Prayer

When they come and pray in this temple; then hear from heaven Your dwelling place, and do according to all for which the foreigner calls to You.   *2 Chronicles 6:32, 33*

God chose the descendants of Abraham, the Israelites, to know Him. But the Creator and Sustainer of all mankind is no nationalistic God. His choice to bless Israel was intended also for the blessing of "all nations," that they too might know Him. Thus, in the dedication of the temple in Jerusalem, King Solomon asked God to listen to the prayers not only of His own people, but to the prayers of the "foreigner, who is not of Your people Israel."

We worship and pray to a universal God. His eyes and ears are open to all who call upon Him in truth. He will hear and answer for He wants "all peoples of the earth to know His name and fear Him." God has a very big heart. He has the whole world in it.

O Father, make us people with spacious hearts. Make the place where we assemble with Your people a house of prayer for all nations.

Inheriting the Nations

Ask of Me, and I will give You the nations for Your inheritance,
and the ends of the earth for Your possession.　　　*Psalm 2:8*

Jesus the Great Intercessor, in His high priestly prayer in John 17, requested of His Father that His disciples would be one, "that the world may know that You have sent Me" (John 17:23). And so it was that the early Church, made one by the Spirit of God and understanding the fulfillment of God's redemptive purposes through His anointed Messiah, prayed: "Give us boldness to speak the word of God." Their intercession joined that of the Great Intercessor, and the Lord heard and answered their request. Filled with the Holy Spirit, they proclaimed the gospel boldly and became witnesses not only to their fellow Jews, but to the Gentiles as well. Nations became the inheritance of the Messiah through them!

Students of Christian missions tell us there are nearly 24,000 distinct "nations" or "people groups" in our world. Let us ask the Lord that for the sake of His Son, Jesus Christ, disciples be made from each of these "nations" and become a part of His inheritance.

Reaching the World

Remember the Lord

All the ends of the world shall remember and turn to the Lord.
Psalm 22:27

"My God, My God, why have You forsaken Me?" The first words of Psalm 22 were uttered by Jesus from the Cross. As the Messiah, the Son of David suffered ridicule, rejection, and suffering as had God's chosen King David a millennium earlier. In David's humiliation was anticipated the greatest humiliation of all, that of God's eternal Son. But His greatest sorrow and grief was that even God forsook Him. Forsook, yes! Forgot, no! God remembered. He has not "hidden His face from Him; but when He cried to Him, He heard."

We live in a world where many feel forsaken and forgotten. Perhaps today you feel this way. Remember again what God has done in Christ! Remember also to "declare His righteousness . . . that He has done this" for those who have not yet heard this good news. Then "all the ends of the world shall remember and turn to the Lord, and all families of the nations shall worship before Him." God remembered! May we remember! For our sakes and for their sakes.

Prosperity and Missions

God be merciful to us and bless us, and cause His face to shine upon us, that Your way may be known on earth.   Psalm 67:1, 2

his psalm begins with the priestly benediction found in Numbers 6:24–26. It was given by the Lord to Moses for Aaron and his sons so they might "put My Name on the children of Israel, and bless them." This blessing included not only peace, but prosperity. The psalmist writes: "Then the earth shall yield her increase; God, our own God, shall bless us" (Ps. 67:6). But it is clear that the material prosperity of God's people was intended to assist in making known His way on earth and His salvation among the nations.

Some wrongly believe that money is the root of all evil. Not so. It is not the amount of money or possessions we have, but how they are used that is right or wrong. God is not against prosperity; He desires to bless His people so His kingdom may expand.

Pray that a spirit of liberality would characterize God's people. May clear understanding of God's purpose for prosperity sweep across the Body of Christ so that God's "way may be known on earth, His salvation among all nations."

King of the Earth

God reigns over the nations.   *Psalm 47:8*

Our God is the ultimate conqueror of all kingdoms. He will be exalted among the nations. Though awesome in power, He is no tyrant. Therefore, all nations are summoned to welcome His enthronement with the clapping of hands and the shouting of victory. Those subdued are invited to "sing praises with understanding" to the king of all the earth.

What a paradox! Our God conquers to liberate. He captures to release. He subdues to free. Personally or nationally, God is the only king who can truly set free. Because sin enslaves, its power must be broken by a greater power, the power of a righteous and holy God. Therefore, we "sing praises with understanding." We recognize that "God reigns over the nations; God sits on His holy throne" (Ps. 47:8). Only He whose throne alone is holy is able to free individuals and nations from the tyranny of sin.

So let's sing His praises with understanding. With the nations, let us clap our hands and shout to God with the voice of triumph! He is our King! He is the King of all kings!

Universal Praise

Let the whole earth be filled with His glory.   Psalm 72:19

So ends the second section of the book of Psalms (chs. 42—72). The entire earth blessing God forever! Unending universal praise is proper for the One who alone does wondrous things! This psalm describes an ideal kingly rule which, to some degree, characterized Solomon's reign in its early years.

The description of the king's rule by the psalmist is a description of God's rule, "who only does wondrous things." The God of Israel alone is the God who judges righteously, bringing peace to His people and justice to the poor. He alone delivers the needy when they cry and redeems them from oppression. Indeed, all "shall be blessed in Him; all nations shall call Him blessed" (Ps. 72:17).

Such a benevolent reign is most fully reflected in God's Son, the Messiah of David's line. He alone fully carries out the will of God. And all who come under His righteous rule begin to enjoy the blessings of God's kingdom. With the psalmist, we cry out "let the whole earth be filled with His glory. Amen and amen."

Worship and Witness

Sing to the Lord, bless His name; proclaim the good news of His salvation from day to day.   Psalm 96:2

Worship and witness flow together. David understood this. In 1 Chronicles 16 David presented a psalm of thanks which was to celebrate the return of the ark of the covenant to Jerusalem. Praise to God for His mighty salvation was to be accompanied by proclamation of this good news among the nations whose gods could not save.

A thousand years later in Jerusalem on the day of Pentecost, people from many nations heard the hundred and twenty Spirit-filled believers speaking in their own languages "the wonderful works of God" (Acts 2:11). Such powerful praise became the occasion for the Apostle Peter to proclaim salvation through Jesus' name to those who had come. With worship came witness, and three thousand believed in Jesus the Messiah and were baptized in water and received the Spirit (Acts 2:38–40).

As those who have likewise experienced "the wonderful works of God," let us, like ancient Israel and the hundred and twenty, both "sing to the Lord" *and* "declare His glory among the nations"!

Reaching the World

Committed to Care

Deliver those who are drawn toward death, and hold back those stumbling to the slaughter.   Proverbs 24:11

Although the exact context is unclear, the point of moral responsibility is clearly evident in this pointed proverb. Those headed for destruction are to be delivered. To plead ignorance does not remove responsibility. Does not God know our hearts? Will He not hold us accountable for the way we failed to care? Sobering questions, indeed!

With the blessing of salvation from destruction, of whatever kind, comes the obligation to rescue others. This is particularly true of salvation from eternal separation from God. Who rescued us but someone who himself had been rescued by hearing about the good news of salvation through Jesus Christ? This is why the Apostle Paul wrote, "I am a debtor both to Greeks and to barbarians, both to wise and to unwise. So, as much as is in me, I am ready to preach the gospel to you who are in Rome also" (Rom. 1:14, 15).

Sixty-five generations have come and gone since Christ returned to heaven. What can and will we do to reach our generation with the gospel? What can and will I do to "deliver those who are drawn toward death"?

Reaching the World

Share Boldly

O Jerusalem, you who bring good tidings, lift up your voice with strength, lift it up, be not afraid.   Isaiah 40:9

"Good news! Tell it boldly!" says the Lord to His servants, the prophets. After seventy years in captivity, they are to proclaim God's message loudly and fearlessly to Israel: "Comfort, my people. Your iniquity is pardoned. Behold, your God! He shall come in strength." Over half a millennium later John the Baptist again speaks these words: "Prepare the way of the Lord; make His paths straight" (Matt. 3:3). Sin's penalty has been paid, its bondage broken.

Yes, "all flesh is grass." Whether in the time of Isaiah or John the Baptist, generations come and generations go, but "the word of our God stands forever" (Is. 40:6–8). It is the eternal word of forgiveness and comfort to all who will repent and believe the gospel of Jesus Christ. But this good news must be declared boldly to each generation before it fades, withers, and passes away as the grass. Therefore, "How beautiful upon the mountains are the feet of him who brings good news" (Is. 52:7).

O Lord, make our feet beautiful and our voices bold . . . today!

Reaching the World

Light to the Nations

I will also give You as a light to the Gentiles, that You should be My salvation to the ends of the earth. Isaiah 49:6

This passage comes from one of the so-called "Servant Songs" in Isaiah. Each of these songs is about Yahweh's servant through whom He will accomplish His redemptive purposes in the world. The nation Israel, as a "kingdom of priests," was chosen to be this servant. But she proved to be an unfaithful witness of God's saving nature and purpose.

Thus, another servant was chosen, one who would do God's will fully. Not only would He restore Israel, He would also be given "as a light to the Gentiles" (Is. 49:6). At Jesus' dedication in the temple, aged Simeon identifies the baby as this light "to bring revelation to the Gentiles, and the glory of Your people Israel" (Luke 2:32).

Now that Jesus, the Light of the world, has returned to heaven, we His people are to be God's light of revelation both to Israel and the nations. The mission of the Messiah is now our mission: "to be a light for the nations, that you may bring salvation to the ends of the earth." How bright is your light? Is it shining to the nations?

Reaching the World

Intercession

*I was speaking, praying, and confessing my sin . . . before the
Lord my God.*   Daniel 9:20

*I*t is marvelous, yet sobering: God invites us to partner with Him, to contend for what He intends. Thus prophetic fulfillment can be conditioned on human response. Daniel is an example. Understanding from Jeremiah's prophecy that seventy years was to be the length of the captivity of God's people (Jer. 25:12; 29:10), Daniel humbled himself to partner in intercessory prayer with this prophecy.

So Daniel writes that "while I was speaking, praying, and confessing my sin and the sin of my people Israel, and presenting my supplication before the Lord my God," the angel Gabriel was sent to release God's redemptive purpose for His people (Dan. 9:20–23). Thus, Israel's return to the Promised Land took place as promised through the prophet Jeremiah.

What if Daniel had not prayed? What if God had found no one to "stand in the gap" (Ezek. 20:30, 31)? Will you be one who partners with God's promises to see the fulfillment of His saving purposes for this generation?

Mercy of God

I know that You are a gracious and merciful God, slow to anger and abundant in lovingkindness, One who relents from doing harm.   *Jonah 4:2*

Jonah is the best known of the Minor Prophets, probably due to the big fish story. But the point of the book is not the big fish but the small-hearted prophet. Jonah was a prophet sent to preach to a Gentile nation. But he ran away! Why?

Believe it or not, Jonah ran away from God's call because he knew what the God of Israel was really like! Why, if he went and preached to those heathen Gentiles, God might save them! And they were the enemy. Surely God would not spare them!

After a second chance, Jonah went, reluctantly. And sure enough, Nineveh repented. God relented. And Jonah was angry. "Should not I pity Nineveh, that great city?" asked God. God loves idolatrous city-dwelling Ninevites.

Do we? Like Jonah, we may know God is "gracious, merciful, slow to anger and abundant in lovingkindness." Are we reflecting His heart toward the hated and violent "Ninevites" in our cities? Are we answering His call to go to them and preach His word of repentance and forgiveness?

Reaching the World

Prayer of Faith

*Though the fig tree may not blossom, nor fruit be on the vines
. . . yet will I rejoice in the Lord.*   *Habakkuk 3:17, 18*

Habakkuk had a problem. He complained to the Lord, "Why are you not judging the violence and injustice in Israel?" God answered, "I am going to do so by using Babylon as My instrument of judgment upon My people!" Now Habakkuk had a bigger problem: "Are you going to use a wicked nation to swallow up those more righteous than themselves?" Again God responds, "Write down the vision. It will certainly happen. I will also judge Babylon. But in the meantime, the just shall live by faith."

Habakkuk's prayer of faith concludes with the verses above. What do you do while you wait for God to deal with violence and injustice in the land? What do you do when all you see around you is desolation and barrenness? You rejoice in the Lord! You take joy in the God of salvation! You live by faith in the One whose righteous purposes *shall* be fulfilled in an unrighteous world when one day all the earth shall keep silence before Him.

God's Priorities

Thus says the Lord of hosts: "Consider your ways!"   *Haggai 1:5*

Nearly two decades had passed since God's people returned from Babylon and laid the foundation of the temple in Jerusalem. The initial opposition that delayed further building had long passed, but the people did not get back to building the temple. They were preoccupied with building their own houses while God's house lay in ruins! Therefore, the Lord sent drought and recession and "blew away" their profits (Hag. 1:9–11).

Haggai calls the people to put first things first, to get back to rebuilding the temple. And they did so in less than a month! Then the drought and recession ended! The Lord had amazing plans for this second temple. Its glory would transcend even Solomon's temple, for into its courts would come the Messiah Himself, and He would bring peace (Hag. 2:6–9; Mal. 3:1).

Today God's dwelling is in His people, not in temples made with human hands. And His people are to include disciples from all the nations. Are we preoccupied with God's priorities or ours? With extending His kingdom or ours? Ask the Lord!

Reaching the World

Sowing the Seed

The field is the world, the good seeds are the sons of the kingdom.
Matthew 13:38

Jesus taught in parables for two reasons: to hide the truth of His kingdom from those who had hard hearts, and to reveal the truth of His kingdom to those who had ears to hear (Matt. 13:10–17). The revelation that "the field is the world, the good seeds are sons of the kingdom" was explained to his disciples. Why? Because they would receive it, even if they did not yet understand it!

Popular thinking was that Israel alone represented the sons of the kingdom and the sons of the wicked one were all non-Jews. Jesus did not come to establish a nationalistic kingdom, but the proclamation of the good news of God's kingdom would result in sons of the kingdom representing not only Israel, but every nation on earth.

How are your ears? Are they ready to hear? Are you ready to grow in your understanding of the universal nature of Christ's kingdom? Are you, like Christ's first disciples, ready to respond and do your part in making disciples of all nations?

Reaching the World

To All Nations

*And this gospel of the kingdom will be preached in all the world
as a witness to all the nations, and then the end will come.*

Matthew 24:14

Jesus outlined the "signs of the times" that will characterize this age as it groans to give birth to the
future age (Matt. 24:3–14). The final "labor pain" is the
universal preaching of the gospel. Then the end will come!

Until the trumpet sounds and Jesus returns to usher in this
wonderful coming age, there is still work to do. Nations
remain that need the witness of the gospel. The twentieth
century is the first century in which the gospel of Jesus
Christ has been preached "in all the world," including
so-called "closed countries." Why then has the Lord not yet
come back? Apparently because this preaching of the
gospel of the kingdom "*in* all the world" must result in a
witness "*to* all nations" (ethnic groups) within these countries.

How are we doing? Of the twenty-four thousand distinct
ethnic groups in the world, about half do not yet have
ongoing "witness" in terms of an indigenous church that
can evangelize the group. "A church for every people
group" is the goal of Christ's words. Let's travail in prayer
toward that end. Amen! Then the end!

Make Disciples

Go therefore and make disciples of all the nations.

Matthew 28:19

*I*ndeed, this is a Great Commission! The main verb of command in the original language is not "go" but "make disciples." Fulfilling the Great Commission requires the making of disciples, not mere deciders. It means baptizing those who believe and teaching them to obey all Christ commanded. Obedience is the goal of Christ's Great Commission. Only doers of His word are true disciples (Matt. 7:21; John 8:31).

There is another way in which this is a Great Commission. Initially Jesus told His disciples to go only to "the lost sheep of Israel" (Matt. 10:6). But now He commands them to go to all the nations (ethnic groups). With true disciples in only about half of the twenty-four thousand "nations," much remains to be done in fulfilling this Great Commission.

Does this sound like "mission impossible"? It would be if it were not for Christ's promise to be with those who go to make disciples in all nations. With the command is the promise. His presence makes it possible.

Miracles

And these signs will follow those who believe. Mark 16:17

*J*esus promised believers He would work with them, "confirming the word through the accompanying signs" (Mark 16:20). Throughout the book of Acts those who spoke the word had it confirmed with miraculous signs and, like Jesus, many believed the good news (Acts 5:12–16; 19:8–12). Unlike the Pharisees, believers did not follow signs; the signs followed them.

Some claim such signs are no longer needed today since we now have the completed Word of God, the Bible. If all that first-century believers had was the living voice of the apostles, and they still needed signs, how much more do we who live in the twentieth century!

Like believers throughout the ages, we need *both* the word of God and the power of God to do the work of God. Anything less is not only sub-biblical, it is ineffective. Therefore, expect miracles! Expect the Lord to confirm His Word with signs as we, like the early disciples, obey His command to "go into all the world and preach the gospel to every creature" (Mark 16:15).

Reaching the World

No Misconceptions

And He opened their understanding, that they might comprehend the Scriptures. Luke 24:45

*B*ible study with the risen Christ! No wonder the disciples' hearts burned within them when Jesus opened their minds to understand the Scriptures (Luke 24:32). From the Law of Moses, the Prophets, and the Psalms He explained two truths they had not really understood. First the Messiah "must suffer and rise from the dead the third day." The popular idea was that when David's offspring, the Messiah, came he would "remain forever," not die (John 12:34). Second, "repentance and remissions of sins would be preached in His name to all nations." The popular idea was that the focus of the Messiah's mission was Israel, not the nations (Acts 1:6).

Therefore, Jesus "opened their minds" to see that the death and rising of the Messiah was taught throughout their Old Testament, and that it was for all nations. What a revelation! A crucified and resurrected Messiah for all nations! Their minds were opened. Their hearts burned. They must tell the world! O Lord, deliver us from popular misconceptions. Open our minds to understand our Bibles. Ignite our hearts to tell our world, "Jesus *is* the Savior for *all* sinners!"

Ready for Harvest

Behold I say to you, lift up your eyes and look at the fields, for they are already white for harvest!   *John 4:35*

A harvest can sneak up on you! Especially when it's a new field! Imagine Jesus, a Jew, a man, a righteous rabbi, talking openly with a Samaritan woman who was immoral and known for her many marriages. But she was thirsty for "living water." So taken was she by Jesus' words, that she went to her village and invited many friends to hear for themselves. With this band of white-robed Samaritans approaching, Jesus pointed out the "whitened harvest" to His Jewish disciples. Many of these despised Samaritans believed in Jesus, exclaiming, "We know that this is indeed the Christ, the Savior of the world" (John 4:42).

Are there any "Samaritans" in our community? Who are the "despised foreigners"? Who are the racial half-breeds? Who are the immoral? Lift up your eyes and look at these unlikely fields. Are they white for harvest? Ask the Lord of the harvest. He knows! Ask Him for a "key contact" like the woman at the well, an influential person with many "friends." It could be harvest time!

Holy Spirit's Power

He breathed on them, and said to them, "Receive the Holy Spirit."

John 20:22

As the Father sent His Son to announce forgiveness, so He sent His disciples to do likewise. Thus, Jesus gave to His followers "the keys of the kingdom" so that "whatever you bind on earth will be bound in heaven, and whatever you loose on earth will be loosed in heaven" (Matt. 16:19).

Forgiveness of sin is "the key" that unlocks the relationship between God and man. Such forgiveness is possible because Jesus died and rose for our sins. We are sent as His ambassadors to announce this good news, proclaiming the forgiveness of sins for those who repent and believe in Him and the retaining of the sins for those who do not. What an awesome task! But through the Spirit's power our words become the word of God as we implore people on Christ's behalf. "Be reconciled to God" (2 Cor. 5:20).

Let Jesus Himself again speak peace to us! Hear and respond to His invitation: "Receive the Holy Spirit." Let Him send us as He was sent by His Father—empowered fully to forgive freely in His Name!

Spirit-Empowered Witness

You shall receive power when the Holy Spirit has come upon you;
and you shall be witnesses to Me.   Acts 1:8

All four Gospel writers record Jesus' final instruc-
tions to take the gospel to the whole world. These
passages now find their climax in Christ's last words before
His return to heaven.

These final words are of utmost importance. As a "last will
and testament" it is to be carried out by those who remain.
Not only did Jesus give authority to carry it out (Matt.
28:18), He also ensured the ability to accomplish the task.
For to "as many as the Lord our God will call" to salvation
is given the "promise of the Father," the gift of the Holy
Spirit (Acts 2:38, 39).

The book of Acts clearly indicates this "internal immersion"
whereby the Spirit gives to every believer the needed
anointing "to be His witnesses." It gives both the motivation and ability to go not only to those close to us culturally and geographically (Jerusalem and Judea), but also to
those far from us culturally and geographically (Samaria
and the end of the earth).

Are we struggling to be "His witness"? Is it difficult "to go"?
Let us ask the Father to renew and release the Spirit's
power in and through us.

Reaching the World

Jesus' Name

There is no other name under heaven given among men by which we must be saved. *Acts 4:12*

The council demanded to know: "By what power or by what name have you done this?" (Acts 4:7). Peter answered, "By the name of Jesus Christ of Nazareth! There is no other name by which we must be saved!" He simply declared what Jesus Himself had said: "I am the way, the truth, and the life. No one comes to the Father except through Me" (John 14:6).

In a world without moral absolutes this sounds narrow-minded. What about sincere Buddhists, Hindus, Muslims and tribal religionists? What is the test of religious truth? It is resurrection from the dead! The historical proof of Jesus' resurrection is unshakable. It is confirmed by the transformed lives of millions of believers.

When the issue is life or death, narrow-mindedness is essential. Who wants a "broad-minded" brain surgeon or airline pilot? If religions could save, why did Jesus bother to come? His very coming clearly and forcefully proclaims: There is no other way to be saved! Yes, the way which leads to life must of necessity be narrow, but it is open to *all* who will call upon His Name. Hallelujah!

Obedience

Through Him we have received grace and apostleship for obedience to the faith among all nations.   *Romans 1:5*

Who can be saved? Only sinners! According to God's standards, there are no righteous people. The Gentiles have not lived up to the light they have in nature and in their conscience (Rom. 1:18–32; 2:12–15). The Jews have not lived up to the light they have in the covenant and the law (Rom. 2:17—3:8). All the world is guilty before God. The issue is a lack of obedience, not a lack of knowledge.

The righteousness God demands is now given freely to all who repent and trust Christ. Will we humbly admit we are sinners and truly turn from our own righteousness? Will we fully trust Christ's righteousness and openly confess Jesus as our Lord? Will we "obey the gospel"?

Why are not all saved? Is it man's lack of light? Is it God's lack of love? It is neither. It is man's lack of obedience. The gospel calls us to obey God's command to repent and to trust Him to save. Therefore, let us "obey the gospel." Then, like Paul, let us call all, whether religious or idolatrous, to the "obedience of faith."

Go and Share

How shall they believe in Him of whom they have not heard?
Romans 10:14

*S*ending . . . proclaiming . . . hearing . . . believing . . . calling. Salvation requires these steps. The first is the most important. Without it the others will not happen. No wonder Paul exclaims "How beautiful are the feet of those who preach the gospel of peace!" (Rom. 10:15). If all upon whom the Spirit comes are Christ's witnesses (Acts 1:8), then all believers are "sent" to bring the good news, first to those within their immediate sphere of influence (Jerusalem). For some it may one day mean being "sent" further to Judea, Samaria, and the end of the earth like the "missionary bands" in the book of Acts (Acts 11:19–21; 13:1–3).

If the Spirit of Christ is in us and He came to seek and to save the lost, how can we do less? May the love of Christ constrain us to go and share the good news, for faith comes by hearing. How else can they hear and believe? How else would we have heard and believed?

Reaching the World

Reaching the Unreached

I have made it my aim to preach the gospel, not where Christ was named, lest I should build on another man's foundation.

Romans 15:20

Paul "planted" the gospel in new territory where others, like Apollos, would then "water" (1 Cor. 3:6). From Jerusalem around to northern Greece, Paul had "fully preached the gospel of Christ" (Rom. 15:19). Now he must find new territory in the western part of the Roman Empire where the gospel had not yet been preached.

Today the challenge of "frontier missions" remains. Over 80 percent of North American Protestant missionaries are, like Apollos, watering seed planted by others. The need is not to redeploy existing missionaries. It is to deploy many new missionaries to peoples yet unreached with the gospel.

Therefore, let's urgently pray the Lord of the harvest to send forth workers into unreached areas, especially the "10/40 window" (bounded from west to east by the Atlantic and Pacific Oceans between 10 and 40 degrees north latitude). Within this "window" are found the vast majority of unreached Muslim, Hindu, and Buddhist groups. Pray for breakthroughs of the gospel with "mighty signs and wonders, by the power of the Spirit of God" (Rom. 15:19).

Reaching the World

Praying for Leaders

Therefore I exhort first of all that supplications, prayers, intercessions, and giving of thanks be made for all men, for kings and all who are in authority.   1 Timothy 2:1, 2

Since the purpose of God our Savior is that all be saved through the ransom of His Son, Paul urges prayer for all men, especially those in authority. Why? Intercession for governing authorities results in a society where "we may lead a quiet and peaceful life in all godliness and reverence." Thus the gospel may be proclaimed more easily and quickly. *Pax Romana* (peace of Rome) characterized the first century and made possible the rapid spread of the gospel throughout the Roman Empire.

Today, as in the first century, the great need is for peace and tranquility in the world. Therefore, a growing number of believers are learning to intercede by name for the kings, presidents, prime ministers, and rulers in each country. Regional conflicts, social unrest, and political upheavals can be quelled and the gospel spread more rapidly as we faithfully petition, pray, and intercede with thanksgiving for all in authority.

Lord, teach us so to pray that Your desire for the salvation of all men may be advanced in every nation in every country.

Reaching the World

God's Final Victory

You were slain, and have redeemed us to God by Your blood out of every tribe and tongue and people and nation. Revelation 5:9

John sees a vision of the ever-expanding worship of heaven around the throne of God. The four living creatures praise God's holiness and the twenty-four elders extol His creative power (Rev. 4:8, 11). Then they begin to sing a "new song" of praise to the Lamb (Rev. 5:9, 10). The angels of heaven join in this new song of praise to the Lamb (Rev. 5:12). Ultimately every creature joins in praise to God and the Lamb saying: "Blessing and honor and glory and power be to Him who sits on the throne, and to the Lamb, forever and ever!" (Rev. 5:13).

What a revelation! Heaven anticipates God's final victory. The Great Commission *will be* fulfilled. The redeemed from every tribe, tongue, people, and nation *will* praise God and the Lamb around the throne. Hallelujah! And in some unexplained way, "the prayers of the saints" played a part (Rev. 5:8). Those redeemed learned to rule and intercede that "His kingdom would come and His will would be done, on earth as it is in heaven." What a revelation! God wins! As we pray!

Jesus' Return

And the Spirit and the bride say, "Come!" And let him who hears say, "Come!" And let him who thirsts come.   Revelation 22:17

Maranatha! "Our Lord, come!" It is the continual cry of the Spirit within the Bride, the Church, for the heavenly Bridegroom. "Jesus, come back!" How earnestly the Bride of Christ longs to be home forever with her Bridegroom!

Maranatha! This cry occasions an equally earnest call. "Let him who thirsts, come." It is the invitation of Christ Himself through His Bride: "If anyone thirsts, let him come to Me and drink" (John 7:37). This "Bridal call" echoes God's generous, yet urgent, call to "come to the waters" of life (Is. 55:1).

Maranatha! Expectation and invitation go together. The Lord's return and world evangelism are vitally connected. With our hands stretched up, we cry, "Our Lord, come!" With our hands stretched out, we call "Come to Jesus!" So ends the book of Revelation and the Bible. And so will such a passionate cry and call end human history! Amen!

Reaching the World

November

The Second Coming

A Prepared Place

I go to prepare a place for you. . . . I will come again and receive you to Myself.
John 14:2, 3

These are among the most comforting words in all of Scripture; from Jesus' own lips, we receive the promise of His return. As the heavenly Bridegroom has preceded the bride, Jesus has faithfully and lovingly prepared an eternal place for us.

In this text Jesus tells us of a *peace,* a *place,* and a *promise.* He begins with a comforting exhortation: do not be troubled; be at peace. Our peace is based on our belief in God's love for us in Jesus Christ. We know that He is trustworthy and that provides us with a foundation of peace upon which to build our lives.

Second, Jesus speaks of a place. He has promised to prepare for us a place where we will have eternal fellowship with Him. Finally, we have His personal promise that He is returning for us. Think of it! His personal signature is on our salvation; because we have received Him, He is coming to receive us!

Second Coming

Until He Comes

This same Jesus, who was taken up from you into heaven, will so come in like manner as you saw Him go into heaven.   Acts 1:11

Before His death, Jesus promised His disciples that not only would He be resurrected, but also that He would return again (John 14:3). Here at His ascension, the promise is reiterated. The angel's words to the disciples seem to imply, "Don't just stand there looking at the sky! Jesus is going to return as He promised, but now you go and do what He told you to do."

There are two very human responses to the promises the Lord has given us. First, we get so caught up in the moment that we lose sight of the promise entirely. In our times of trial or feverish activity, the promise of God's good work in us is simply set aside. Second, we can become so captivated by God's promise for our future that we neglect the tasks He has given us today, which are to become the pathway for the fulfillment of all He has promised.

Today be reminded, Jesus is coming again! There is much to be done to prepare ourselves and to reach the world around us in His love.

Second Coming

Jesus' Return

For the Lord Himself will descend from heaven with a shout,
with the voice of an archangel, and with the trumpet of God. . . .

1 Thessalonians 4:16

You will not be able to miss Jesus' return. There will be a *three-fold announcement:* Jesus is going to shout from heaven, and all those who belong to Him will hear His voice; the voice of an archangel will be heard announcing to every creature that the King of glory has now come to claim His possession; and the trumpet will sound so clearly and with such force that the dead in Christ will be awakened.

Also in this passage are *three precious promises.* The dead in Christ shall rise; those loved ones who have preceded us in Christ will be included in this day of all days. Next, those who are alive will meet the Lord in the air—a face to face reunion with Jesus and all those most dear to us. Lastly, we shall always be with our Savior.

The day of His coming is more precious with each passing moment. Look up! Your redemption is drawing near. Listen! One day the air will be filled with that glorious announcement: Jesus is here!

Second Coming

With Watchful Heart

Watch therefore, for you know neither the day nor the hour in which the Son of Man is coming. Matthew 25:13

Throughout history believers have tried to determine when the Lord will return, and an ignorance of the history of this folly has led some in every decade to presume to pinpoint the time of Jesus' coming. Some have speculated that since we do not know the hour or the day, we may be able to pinpoint the month or year of His return. That completely misses the point of God's dealing with us concerning His return. Jesus tells us directly that no one but the Father knows the time.

Jesus begins this verse with a command: "Watch." The challenge the Lord gives us is to be constantly and eagerly waiting for His return. Therefore, our duty is two-fold: to prepare ourselves for His coming, so that the Lord will receive a bride "without spot or wrinkle" (Eph. 5:27); and to "do business" until He returns, so that the kingdom of God is preserved and extended on earth (Luke 19:13).

As we await Jesus' return, let us be about the Father's business.

Second Coming

Our Blessed Hope

He who testifies to these things says, "Surely I am coming quick-
ly." Amen. Even so, come, Lord Jesus!   Revelation 22:20

Jesus' last words in all of Scripture are dramatically placed so that all who believe can never forget, "I am coming quickly." This promise from the Savior's lips has come to us in God's Word through the pens of the prophets, the voices of angels, and the teachings of the apostles. This promise has been found throughout the Old Testament and is the blessed hope of the New Testament (Titus 2:13). God's covenant promise to His people is that one day eternity will once again intersect humanity, but this time we will always be with the Lord.

These final words of Jesus in Scripture were delivered to a first-century church beleaguered by false prophets and persecution, which led to martyrdom in the Coliseum in Rome. It was the devil's vicious attempt to snuff the infant beginning of the Lord's church. Jesus' words brought hope then, and they still do. Regardless of the current trial of your life, do not let this hope be overshadowed: Jesus is coming quickly!

Second Coming

Faithful Stewardship

Do business till I come. *Luke 19:13*

The truth of this parable in Luke is sobering. A nobleman has given resources to certain ones in his realm to manage in his absence. Upon his return he commands that an accounting be made of all the money that was placed in their charge. To those who earned profit, there was great reward; both were given cities to rule. But to the one who buried the money, who simply returned what he had been given, his money was taken from him with a rebuke from his lord.

We do not know the day or time of the Lord's return, but each of us has been given gifts, resources, and talents to further the advance of God's kingdom. Our salvation does not depend on what we do with those gifts; however, the furthering of the kingdom of God in our world does. The Lord is coming again, and He will reward those who respond with faithful stewardship and boldness in ministry for Him. Let the gifts He has given you find their fullest fruit, multiplying blessing in His kingdom and producing unequivocal joy in your life.

Second Coming

Living Soberly

We should live soberly, righteously, and godly in the present age.
Titus 2:12

"*Soberly*" in the original language is an interesting combination of two Greek words: *sodzo,* to save, and *phren,* the mind. Literally, the Apostle Paul is telling Titus to live with a "saved mind."

So often the concept of sobriety is linked with the English word "somber"; we ascribe to it a gloominess which was completely foreign to the Apostle Paul's thinking. The following verse reminds us that we are "looking for the blessed hope and glorious appearing of our great God and Savior Jesus Christ" (Titus 2:13). But He is not returning for a repressed, grim church. He is coming back for a vital, joyful, industrious bride who has prepared herself with the understanding that the hour demands prudence and her Lord requires a bride who is in full possession of her emotional and intellectual faculties.

We are called to live as examples of God's redemptive work in the midst of a perverse and dying generation. Our sobriety points the way to salvation for others who desperately need for themselves what Jesus has done in us.

Second Coming

Jesus Serves Us

Blessed are those servants whom the master, when he comes, will find watching.
Luke 12:37

The signs of Jesus' coming are everywhere; this is the season to watch faithfully for the Lord's return. It is Jesus who declares "blessed" over those who watch for Him. And, it is in this same verse that Jesus promises "he (the returning master) will gird himself and have them sit down to eat, and will come and serve them."

When Jesus returns He promises to feed us Himself, filling every emptiness that can only be satisfied with a feast provided by His own hand. Wherever we have hungered we will be completely filled.

He further promises that He will be the One to serve us. The thought of Jesus girding Himself as a house servant for us is incomprehensible. He has already given us so much! How much more could He give after He poured out His life for us and sent His Spirit to us?

So great is His love, so real is His promise, and so soon is His coming.

Second Coming

Prepare and Watch

The day of the Lord will come as a thief in the night.
2 Peter 3:10

A thief gains his advantage by striking when people least expect it, and the thought of a burglar breaking into our house while we sleep is terrifying. We try to secure ourselves against this possibility with double dead-bolt locks, bars on the windows, burglar alarms, and more police. Jesus promised us that the day of the Lord would come suddenly, and this "thief in the night" cannot be stopped. There is no defense against the supernatural day of His coming!

But unlike thieves in our world, Jesus will only take what is already His.

Only those who disregard Jesus' warning have any need to be concerned. Fear has no place for those who are prepared.

People are also victimized by the thief when they carelessly leave themselves unprotected. Scripture declares that people in pursuit of their own pleasures, living life indifferently to its consequence, open themselves to the destruction of the ultimate thief, the devil.

As we heed Jesus' warning, let us prepare ourselves for His coming, "looking for and hastening the coming of the day of God" (2 Pet. 3:12).

Second Coming

Holy Conduct

What manner of persons ought you to be in holy conduct and godliness . . . ?   2 Peter 3:11

The Apostle Peter is prophesying concerning Christ's return and the events surrounding the end of the world. He declares that our world "will be dissolved" and that the "elements will melt with fervent heat." This complete undoing of our physical world leaves an important question: How should we live?

The answer is an immediate "in holy conduct and godliness." Everything else will dissolve, burn, or melt away. Carnal desires and compromised lifestyles fixed to the condemned structures of our fallen world will not stand before the presence of the returning Son of God who is all righteousness and holiness. All the material acquisition, status, and symbols of human accomplishment will vanish. And the portion of our lives that are built on the wood, hay, and straw of pursuits without eternal value will be consumed (1 Cor. 3:13).

We are called to live in the hope of His coming, not to dread His judgment. Instead, let us build our lives in obedience to His Word so that our conduct reveals our love for Jesus and opens the way for others to love Him too.

Second Coming

Keep This Commandment

*Keep this commandment without spot, blameless until our Lord
Jesus Christ's appearing.*   1 Timothy 6:14

The Apostle Paul is writing to his beloved spiritual son,
Timothy, offering fatherly advice—"keep this commandment." Referring to more than the immediately preceding verse, Paul's encouragement is to keep all the commandments that have been given to this emerging spiritual leader so that God's blessing will continue on his life and
ministry.

In 1 John 3:23 this commandment is taught in its most
potent and definable terms, that "we should believe on the
name of [God's] Son Jesus Christ and love one another, as
He gave us commandment." We lay claim to His name,
because He has laid claim to us. Pressing on in faith the
kingdom of God advances, pushing back every work of
darkness that destroys men. Loving each other we fulfill
the mission of the Savior who has unlimited love for His
people and a passion for sinners that compelled Him to
sacrifice His life.

"[Keeping] this commandment" guarantees our faithful
witness and releases His abounding blessing in our lives.
"Until our Lord Jesus Christ's appearing" calls us to ongoing obedience and steadfastness of faith without compromise.

Second Coming

Abide in Him

Abide in Him, that when He appears, we may have confidence and not be ashamed before Him at His coming.   1 John 2:28

We want to be ready when Jesus returns, but what are we supposed to do? Here is the answer: Be with Jesus everyday. If we have been conscious of living in the Lord's presence day by day, then we are abiding in Him. If we measure our words and our daily walk to be pleasing to Him, then when He returns we will not be ashamed and His coming will be the return of a friend.

Abiding in Him, the Apostle John gently reminds us, is demonstrated by the ongoing work of the Holy Spirit producing a changed life. As we live with Jesus, there is an unmistakable proof of our being with a righteous and loving Savior. That proof is "that everyone who practices righteousness is born of Him" (1 John 2:29). The profession of our faith in Christ is proved by the pursuit of the practice of righteousness. It is in this pursuit that we have confidence in the day of His coming and in knowing that there is no shame for those who "abide in Him."

Second Coming

A Bright Coming

The lawless one will be revealed, whom the Lord will consume with the breath of His mouth and destroy with the brightness of His coming.   2 Thessalonians 2:8

The lawless one comes with Satan's "power, signs, and lying wonders" (2:9), but it is no match for the Lord's return in almighty power. The same breath that spoke the creation into being and breathed life into Adam will now consume God's enemies. All of hell's power will be overthrown when Jesus returns, and in the "brightness of His coming" there dawns a new day for all of God's people.

The ultimate fulfillment of that new day awaits Jesus' second coming to earth, when all hell's power will finally be ended. But the new day can begin for every believer today. Jesus comes with almighty power to consume the adversaries of our souls, that draw us into sin and ceaselessly torment. Though Jesus waits for the day and hour of the Father's release to win back the planet, He won the battle for us at the cross in His first coming. Invite Him, today, to vanquish the forces of hell so that we may experience "the brightness of His coming" in our personal worlds.

Signs

Now when these things begin to happen, look up and lift up your heads, because your redemption draws near. Luke 21:28

When Jesus returns to earth, there will be signs of His coming. There will be signs in the sun, moon, and stars—ozone depletion, global warming, greenhouse gases. There will be distress among nations—the collapse of communism, Middle East unrest, and crises in international economics. There will be the failing of men's hearts for fear—AIDS, unemployment, collapse of the family. But Jesus said that when all "these things begin to happen, look up and lift up your heads, because your redemption draws near."

Every generation of Christians, beginning with the first century, have believed that Jesus would return in their lifetime. The headlines in the newspapers change, and the crises facing man continue to grow. But the answer is always the same: "Look up and lift up your heads." The answer for man's need will never be found in technological breakthrough, political change, or social evolution. Earth's needs can only be answered by heaven's resource. So let us keep our eyes fixed heavenward as we continue living for Jesus and loving the world. He is coming back with power and great glory, very soon.

Second Coming

Victory over Death

But thanks be to God, who gives us the victory through our Lord Jesus Christ.   *1 Corinthians 15:57*

There is a final victory for all of us in Jesus Christ. This victory will cheat the ultimate force that terrifies man. This victory will be registered in cemeteries all over the world. This victory will be so total and will happen so quickly, in a heartbeat, that nothing can stop it. Death will finally be conquered. "In the twinkling of an eye" (v. 52) it will be over. The Lord of life will claim His own.

There will be a blast from the "last trumpet of heaven," the sound of an eternal coronation for the King of kings. The resounding ring of this last trumpet will herald the breaking open of the sky, the raising of the dead in Christ, and the final overthrow of the devil's last hope, death itself. There is a victory ahead; it awaits all who call on the name of the Lord. "Death is swallowed up in victory. O Death, where is your sting? O Hades, where is your victory?" (1 Cor. 15:54, 55). For Jesus, the Lord of life, will come and nothing can stop Him!

Second Coming

Ultimate Redemption

To those who eagerly wait for Him He will appear a second time, apart from sin, for salvation.   Hebrews 9:28

Jesus came the first time as a babe in a manger and grew up to be the Savior on a cross. He was "offered" by Father God for our sin. The word *prosphero* (offer) is a compound of two Greek words, *pros* (toward) and *phero* (to bring). In addition to the more literal sense of bringing or leading to, the word denotes an offering, whether of gifts, prayer, or sacrifices. So Jesus came the first time bringing a gift, a sacrifice for the sins of many.

His second coming will be radically different. Our sin completely sacrificed for, He will come to finish what he has begun. What has begun with the forgiveness of sin for all who believe will be consummated in the ultimate redemption of the planet to Himself. All history pivots on the moment of His return, and the complete work of salvation will become evident. The cleansing of the earth, the final transport to heaven for all who believe, the drying of every tear, the ending of every pain—salvation completely fulfilled will be upon us.

Second Coming

Prepare and Watch

Blessed is he who watches, and keeps his garment, lest he walk naked and they see his shame.   *Revelation 16:15*

The garment to which Jesus refers has nothing to do with being "dressed for success." The Laodiceans in Revelation 3:18 were rich and had fine clothes, but Jesus spoke directly, "Buy from Me . . . white garments, that you may be clothed." Man's attempts to cover himself began in the Garden of Eden with inadequate fig leaves. It continues today with a multi-billion dollar fashion industry. But none of it can cover man's nakedness which is revealed in sin. The desperation by which man attempts to hide himself from God and convince himself of his own sufficiency shall all fall away on the day Jesus returns.

He will never shame us. He is a God of love and mercy, and He gives to us garments that are clean and acceptable. But it is our job to keep those garments on. Repentance for sin, staying current on attitudes and relationships, and an open heart toward Him keeps us "dressed" for the day He returns.

Patience

Establish your hearts, for the coming of the Lord is at hand.

James 5:8

The testing of faith produces patience, which is the hallmark of a mature believer. Only under the pressure of trial can the believer test the true depth of his faith in God. The established heart will not waver, but will rejoice in the goodness of God.

We have all been there. On our way to some distant location a little voice from the back seat of the car demands, "How long till we're there?" It makes no difference to that child if the question was answered only two minutes before. He wants to know NOW! He is anxious to get there and uncomfortable in the back seat, and every moment of a trip seems endless.

The same feelings hold true for those growing to maturity in Christ. We know the promise of His coming and the indescribable joy of eternity with Him. We also experience the trial of today and look forward to the reward of tomorrow. Be patient! Establish your heart! He is coming soon enough, and His people will not be disappointed.

Second Coming

Our Reward

Then He will reward each according to his works.

Matthew 16:27

Jesus had just taught His disciples that each person must "take up his cross and follow Me" (v. 24). He declared that human effort to save our lives results in death and surrendering our lives to Him will bring salvation. In these razor-like remarks, the Lord cuts a clear path for His disciples to walk. It requires their understanding and acceptance that true discipleship means forsaking all selfish ambition. No longer does righteousness consist of observing an external legal code. Righteousness is now defined by the Person of Jesus and not by the Law. This Person, who is righteousness incarnate, requires our loyalty. True discipleship requires total commitment without distraction or compromise.

With this wholehearted pursuit of discipleship, Jesus promises a reward at His return. God is faithful to remember our service of love. And though our entrance into heaven has to do with our faith in Christ alone, His future reward to us is based on our fidelity, obedience, and service—today.

God Will Judge

And He will separate them one from another, as a shepherd
divides his sheep from the goats. Matthew 25:32

The Lord's return will usher in a judgment based on moral character. This character is revealed by the presence of charitable deeds or the lack of them. The verses following this text give a picture of compassionate response to human suffering and need. Jesus declares that any good work done to those who hurt is good work done unto Him. The outward evidence of our good works demonstrates inner righteousness or unrighteousness. Good works do not produce good character; good character produces good works.

Ephesians 2:10 further elaborates this truth. "We are His workmanship, created in Christ Jesus for good works." Before faith in Christ, our good works, however noble, offer no relief for man's ultimate need—forgiveness of sin. However, having received forgiveness through faith in Christ, the Holy Spirit begins a transformation in us that makes good works a byproduct of our faith. James challenges us to "be doers of the word, and not hearers only" (1:22).

Let us live as transformed people, serving with compassion the needy world around us.

Second Coming

Respond and Repent

. . . who will both bring to light the hidden things of darkness and reveal the counsels of the hearts.   *1 Corinthians 4:5*

This is light-years beyond Santa Claus declaring "who's naughty or who's nice." Our actions will be matched with our motives. The counsel of the heart will be the measuring device for every action. It is not good enough to do the right thing; we are accountable for our thoughts and attitudes as well.

I used to fear that God would know my true motives (as if I could hide them in the first place). I simply did not understand His great love for me. Everyday the Holy Spirit is at work drawing me to a closer walk with the Lord. The "still, small voice" that speaks to all of us is leading us to a purity of heart and motive.

As the Holy Spirit uncovers attitudes and motives, simply respond in faith; repent and move on! It is His grace that has brought us this far, and it will be His greatest joy to complete the good work He has begun in us until the day He returns (Phil. 1:6).

Second Coming

Preach the Word

I charge you therefore before God and the Lord Jesus Christ . . .
Preach the word!   *2 Timothy 4:1, 2*

*P*aul underscores the urgency of his message with the phrase "I charge you." The Greek word for "charge" is used in connection with a solemn and emphatic testimony in a court of law. We must be ready to minister the Word of the Lord boldly and courageously, now! Timothy is charged with defending God's Word tirelessly, being careful to communicate truth with absolute accuracy, because "the time will come when they will not endure sound doctrine, but according to their own desires . . . they will turn their ears away from the truth, and be turned aside to fables" (vv. 3, 4).

There is a "window of opportunity" for the gospel to be heard and responded to by every person. There also is a relentless adversary beguiling, bullying, and bending the truth so that those who are lost will not respond. The time to share is now, while people have ears to hear. The day of His return draws near, hearts will grow harder, and ears will grow dull. Let us minister the Word now, while we can still be heard.

Second Coming

The Judgment

The Lord comes with ten thousands of His saints, to execute judgment on all, to convict all who are ungodly.
Jude 14, 15

Jude, the brother of James and the brother of our Lord, makes an uncompromising declaration: sinners will be judged. The word "sinner" (Greek, *hamartolos*) is used for an archer missing the target or for a traveler leaving the familiar road and taking twisted paths that cause him to lose his way. The word denotes one devoted to sin by choice, a transgressor whose thoughts, words, and deeds are contrary to God's eternal laws.

This passage teaches us that each person's deeds, ways, and words must be accounted for. The terrifying and inescapable truth is that Jesus is returning to judge sinners. But for the believer, the blessed promise becomes eternal hope—"So great is His mercy toward those who fear Him; as far as the east is from the west, so far has He removed our transgressions from us" (Ps. 103:11, 12).

It is we who sin, but it is He who removes that which would eternally cling to us. We need not fear; the Lord who saves us now will keep us at His return.

Second Coming

Sanctification

May the God of peace Himself sanctify you completely.
1 Thessalonians 5:23

It is an incredible promise: If we will allow it, God Himself will sanctify us! When we think of all that needs to be done in our lives, we begin to wonder exactly what it will take to blast the resistance of our flesh into sanctification before the Lord. We want to live the holiness of life in the Lord, but our fears say that it will take prolonged, spiritual warfare to subjugate our carnal man. In contrast, the text goes on to say that when the God of peace has completed His work there will be a total transformation, "spirit, soul, and body."

The saying goes, "God loves you too much to leave you the way you are." It is true! He is not asking us to start a self-help program, become more sincere, or struggle toward perfection. He is perfection! If we will allow His life to grow in us, then we will truly be sanctified and blameless at His coming.

Second Coming

Citizens of Heaven

For our citizenship is in heaven, from which we also eagerly wait for the Savior, the Lord Jesus Christ. *Philippians 3:20*

Paul writes while confined in prison awaiting Roman justice. As a Roman citizen he had all the privileges of travel, the protection of the legal system, and the right of appeal to Caesar himself (Acts 25:11), the undisputed emperor of the known world. Yet, Paul reminds us that our ultimate citizenship has nothing to do with human affairs, national allegiance, or cultural heritage. We who have been born again have received a passport from heaven, and regardless of the path we journey today, our ultimate destination is assured.

We eagerly await the Lord's coming so that we may be transported to our journey's end. The riot of confusion we witness in our world, and the tragedy and devilish cruelty which so marks our earthly existence and is verified everyday in the headlines of every newspaper and broadcast, reminds us that we are simply passing through. Our destination is heaven, and at Jesus' return He will take us there.

Second Coming

Christ's Appearance

*When Christ who is our life appears, then you also will appear
with Him in glory.*
                                                    Colossians 3:4

The Apostle Paul reminds us that before our salvation
we were "dead in trespasses and sins" (Eph. 2:1), but
now Jesus is our life. And when He appears we will appear
with Him. *Phaneroo* is the Greek word for "appear," and it
means to lay bear, uncover, make visible, to make known
what has been hidden or unknown. It describes Christ's
appearing, when we will see Him in the full expression of
His glorious character. We will not just see the King of
kings in the clouds. We will see the God of glory revealed
in all of His love, mercy, justice, and power.

The same word applies to us. We "will appear with Him in
glory." However, what is to be revealed in us is the work
that the Holy Spirit has performed in us. As we have "set
[our] mind on things above," as we have "hidden" our life
in Christ, died to our fleshly desires, and "put on the new
man" in Christ (Col. 3:2–10), we will bear striking resem-
blance to the Lord with whom we will appear.

Second Coming

Crowns of Glory

When the Chief Shepherd appears, you will receive the crown of glory that does not fade away.   *1 Peter 5:4*

The Chief Shepherd is coming to reward those who have faithfully served His flock. Those who are witness of the sufferings of Christ will also partake of the "glory that will be revealed" (v. 1). These leaders will receive a crown which signifies their triumph over obstacles and their fidelity to the people of their mission and call. This crown is not the garland worn by military victors or athletes in the games. Those laurels wither, fade, and are forgotten with the next military campaign or the next victor in the games. The Lord's rewards are eternal.

"God is not unjust to forget your . . . labor of love which you have shown toward His name, in that you have ministered to the saints, and do minister" (Heb. 6:10). The Lord Jesus, who gives gifts of ministries to serve His body (Eph. 4:11), cares deeply and rewards richly those who have chosen to serve. Do not weary in the call. The Lord sees our service, knows our struggle, and He is faithful to remember.

Second Coming

Made Like Jesus

We know that when He is revealed, we shall be like Him.

1 John 3:2

There is a two-part miracle that happens to make us like Jesus. It begins when we open ourselves to His life as our Savior. We are born again in an instant, translated from death to life. And like any newborn, when we start growing, we look like our parents! Second Corinthians 3:18 declares we "are being transformed into the same image from glory to glory, just as by the Spirit of the Lord." As long as we live, this process of growth towards maturity takes place.

The second stage of our transformation will occur at His return: "when He is revealed, we shall be like Him." Instantly, "in the twinkling of an eye," everything of our corruptible, mortal existence will give way to incorruptible immortality, just like our Lord (1 Cor. 15:52). The Lord will accomplish this final stage of the process. We partner with Him in growth, but He sovereignly transforms the rest at His coming. And, "we shall be like Him."

Second Coming

Live for Jesus

I am not ashamed of the gospel of Christ, for it is the power of
God to salvation. *Romans 1:16*

The world tries to intimidate us with intellectual arguments against faith in Christ. Society attempts to silence us with the "shame" of our refusal to surrender to the valueless pursuit of greedy pleasure. Living for Jesus is foolishness to those who are perishing in their sin. There is no compromise. The world rejects all but its own. And those born into the kingdom of God find themselves at odds with a world that knows no king but their own selfish desire.

Our rejection of the world has to do with its standards, values, priorities, and deeds. Our love for the world is based on the worth of each human being created in the image of God. We must reach our family and neighbors with God's love. To do this we become "all things to all men" (1 Cor. 9:22) without capitulating to compromise. Jesus is our Lord. Let everyone know the glorious truth of His life and salvation.

Second Coming

Rest

. . . to give you who are troubled rest with us when the Lord Jesus is revealed from heaven with His mighty angels.

2 Thessalonians 1:7

When the Lord returns there will be a visitation of God's glory. This glory will consume God's adversaries and give blessed rest to those who have labored long for Him. In the struggle against evil, amid constant din of a chaotic world, and from the hardships of being strangers in a foreign land, God's people need the rest He will bring.

But we don't have to wait until His coming to find rest. There is hope today for refreshment in the midst of the grind of our daily pressures. "With stammering lips and another tongue He will speak to this people, to whom He said, 'This is the rest with which you may cause the weary to rest'" (Is. 28:11, 12).

Living in the fullness of the Spirit until He comes again is the answer to the relentless pressure of today which seeks to overwhelm us. Live full of the Spirit; worship with your spiritual language; and rejoice in His coming when our final rest in Christ will come.

Second Coming

December

Gifts of the Holy Spirit

Christmas Visitation

The Dayspring from on high has visited us. Luke 1:78

Has it occurred to you that God foresaw the eventual worldwide celebration His Son's birth would bring about? He did! Contrary to the debunker's refusal to enjoy a holy spirit of celebration, God seems to delight in creating festive times for His people. An entire "string of lights," so to speak, was assembled by Him in the Old Testament where He ordered feast-times on an average of every two or three months!

Of course, carnal and commercial celebrations miss the point of Christmas—we all know and acknowledge that. But do not let the Scrooge spirit overthrow the Holy Spirit's desire to awaken fresh expectancy and joy in your heart at this precious season.

God has visited us! That "the Word became flesh" brought about a new day. "Dayspring" means "dawn," and as we approach Christmas this year, do so by welcoming the Holy Spirit's rise with fresh joy, hope, and love.

Gifts of the Holy Spirit

Christmas Visitation

When the fullness of time had come, God sent forth His Son.
Galatians 4:4

*G*od keeps a calendar. It isn't controlled by human pressure nor limited to earth's perspective. It is governed in the light of His love for each of us individually and the entire race collectively.

The Bible makes this singular observation: God sent His Son right on time. That's what "the fullness of time" means; there was a heavenly ordained and appointed moment for the Redeemer's dramatic entry. That's why we celebrate Christmas—to worship and rejoice again in the mighty love and overarching care for mankind which planned, calendared this visitation from heaven.

Just as we calendar our visits to those we love or to those who need our presence and help, the Father's gift of His Son was calendared to bring about a visit which answered human need. And best of all, the Holy Spirit keeps the power of that "visitation" flowing currently. This Christmastime, let Him bring the blessing of a special Christmas visit to you!

Christmas Visits

What is man . . . that You visit him? Psalm 8:4

How often have you watched the glistening eyes of a child as Christmastime lights are arrayed and the little one stares in happy awe at the splendor surrounding him? In a more mature way, that is exactly what stirred David's soul—the lights were the stars, and his awestruck joy was born of gratitude to the Creator.

As he sings, studying the night sky as a beginning point in praising God for the whole of His created universe, David comes to a focus in it all. He basically says, "Lord, when I look at all this, I am overwhelmed with one question: What is man that you pay so much attention to him?"

God's "Christmas visit" to mankind is the ultimate statement He has made about us. His visit not only unfolds His *love reaching,* but unveils the sense of value He places on each of us and His *love redeeming*—seeking to restore our loss. As His children, may the lights of Christmas shine in our eyes with gratitude for such love.

Christmas Visits

Behold, wise men from the East came to Jerusalem.   Matthew 2:1

Jesus Christ's coming to earth is the entry point of salvation's beginning for mankind. It's right that we celebrate Christmas! Even though it is true that no one can actually mark the day on which Jesus was born; and even though some object that the season we celebrate was once a pagan feast, it is still right to celebrate! After all, since we do not know the exact day, neither do we know but that Christmas Day *is* the right day. And if pagans corrupted the season in times past, our holy rejoicing can reclaim it with praise to God now!

The ancient sages, the wise men from the East, are the ones who made the longest "Christmas visit," geographically speaking. And the fact that they are memorialized in the pages of God's eternal Word should tell us something about how God values the efforts of "people who make a big thing out of Christmas."

Let the wise men teach us wisdom. God has visited us from out of eternity. Set a course to "meet Christmas" by making a special visit yourself. You can start by calling on the Lord—for a special Christmas-work in your heart.

Christmas Visits

Let us now go to Bethlehem. Luke 2:15

Christmas sets everyone on the move. It does that today, as travel reaches record proportions, but it all started long before now. When God comes to earth, all earth is set in motion!

The shepherds experienced a supernatural encounter which made it impossible for them to remain as they were or where they were. In response to the angels' visit they planned a visit to the manger—an *awakening* visit became a *seeking* visit.

We may be wise to learn from their response. Maybe we all need to say, in a new way, "Let us now go to Bethlehem." Let us allow this Christmas season to capture our souls with the marvel of Jesus' coming. Open your heart to the Holy Spirit and allow Him to bring you—as the shepherds—to a new place of supernatural encounter with God.

And as He begins this, even now in this prayer-filled moment, let us each one plan to follow through. Relive the practical good sense of the shepherds, saying, "I'm not going to just sit through Christmas. I'm going to my appointed Bethlehem." He's waiting to meet you there.

Gifts of the Holy Spirit

Visited with Hope

Do not be afraid . . . for your prayer is heard.   *Luke 1:13*

Nothing seemed to bring hopelessness to a home in the ancient world like childlessness. If a couple had no children, a shadow seemed to hang over the home, as though God was displeased with them.

Such was the home of Zacharias and Elizabeth, both of whom the Bible reveals as being full-hearted in their dedication and service to the Lord. Their childlessness was certainly no reflection of divine displeasure—but how were they to be sure?

Somehow their plight mirrors many of us who face barren circumstances and wonder if we might have drifted outside the circle of divine blessing. But the beauty of this text's story (Luke 1:5–25) is how God answered their heartcry for a child by a miraculous restoration of Elizabeth's childbearing ability. Further, their son's birth becomes, if you will, a steppingstone to Christmas. The conception of John the Baptist in his mother Elizabeth's womb begins a trail of events leading to Jesus' birth and ministry. Answered prayer, the renewal of hope, barrenness overcome. It's Christmastime!

Visited with Silence

But when he came out, he could not speak.   Luke 1:22

The angel's "visiting" a temporary specialness upon him may not have seemed a blessing to Zacharias. But after receiving the promise that Elizabeth would have a child, his doubt prompts the angel Gabriel to take that action. He says, "Because you did not believe, you will be without speech until the child is born" (vv. 13–22).

Some may consider this a punishment, but it involves a greater idea than vindictiveness for unbelief. Rather, the angel's action is an oblique lesson in the amazing power of our speech. As beings made in His image, God has granted to us, His own people, the privilege of "laying hold of" or "claiming" His promises. Our speaking what God has said is a very real means of bringing the power of His Word to bear upon life's specific situations.

The opposite is also true. Doubt has the power to annul the potential of a promise, at least insofar as it might have applied to us. Thus, the angel neutralized Zacharias' ability to express doubt until the promised baby was born. This Christmastime may be a season to learn the power of silence to neutralize doubt, and the power of praise to receive God's works of grace.

Gifts of the Holy Spirit

Visited with the Incredible

For with God nothing will be impossible.   *Luke 1:37*

This much-quoted verse is seldom linked with the Christmas story, but it lies at its center. The statement was made to Mary, as she was receiving the most incredible promise ever given to a human being concerning physical possibilities. "You (a virgin) shall have a child, and the child will be God's Son!"

Of course we revel in this marvelous invasion of our world with the mercy-gift of Jesus the Savior. His miraculous entry, via the virgin birth, is an overwhelming mystery and a profound article of our faith. But Christ's miraculous birth into the world is not only a *physical* fact fulfilled in the past; it is also a *spiritual* possibility today!

Just as Christ was presented to the world in a physical way through Mary, the Lord Jesus wants to be presented to the world in a mighty, spiritual way today through you and me! "Wait," we might say with Mary, "How can this be?" And the answer is the same to us as to her: "The power of the Holy Spirit shall come upon you!" Thus, the miracle of Christmas is repeated, in a new way—over and over, as we are visited with the incredible gift of "Christ in you, the hope of glory" (Col. 1:27).

Gifts of the Holy Spirit

Visited To Be Visiting

Now Mary . . . went into the hill country with haste. Luke 1:39

There is a seldom noticed yet preciously tender lesson to be found in Mary's actions immediately following the angel's visit announcing her role as bearer of the Christ Child. She had been told that her cousin Elizabeth was also experiencing an unusual, though different, visitation of God's grace: that now, late in life, she was in the sixth month of pregnancy with her first child (1:36).

Now, almost immediately after she has discovered that she, Mary of Nazareth, is about to become the most unique woman in history, notice how beautifully her attention turns from herself to a need where she can serve. She travels to help Elizabeth, and verse 56 says that Mary stayed with her aged relative and served her until Elizabeth's baby was delivered.

This could well become our most important Christmas lesson for this year. Mary demonstrates a principle of God's love in action: May I be more concerned to assist the fulfillment of what the Lord is doing in another person than I am with what He is doing in me.

Gifts of the Holy Spirit

God's Giving Ways

Every good gift . . . comes down from the Father.   James 1:17

A man, feeling it his duty to deride the practice of giving presents at Christmas, was angrily assailing another Christian for doing so. To this the gift-giving Christian responded, "I can't help it. It was God's idea before it was mine!"

As we cherish the memory of God's gift-giving ways, and the gift of His Son Jesus to our world this season, it is the most appropriate of times to think on this aspect of the Father's nature. He's a Giver! And since His qualities of character are certainly desirable to see mature in ours, an unselfish and loving spirit of gift-giving is a grace to learn year-round.

Capture all this text points to of God's unchanging, season-less habit of giving: "Every good gift and every perfect gift is from above, and comes down from the Father of lights [sounds like Christmas!], with whom there is no variation [His changeless nature is to give] or shadow of turning [literally, no difference from season to season]."

Gifts of the Holy Spirit

The Father's Gifts

God has dealt to each one a measure of faith. Romans 12:3

These words preface a list of gifts that our Father and Creator has given in varied measures and groupings to human beings. The seven categories noted in Romans 12:6–8 have sometimes been called "the motivating gifts" of God. In other words, God has given everyone "a measure of faith," that is, a beginning point for responding to His will for them. This starting point is activated as each person realizes and uses the unique and distinct gift he has; when each of us serves others by acting on those inclinations which God has placed within to motivate our vocations and our ministries to others.

In this December season, come before Father God with both gratitude and teachableness—gratitude, first, to thank Him for the fact He has invested something of His creative potential in us; then teachableness, saying, "Father, show me more about how the gifts You have given me (some of which I may not even yet recognize or acknowledge) might glorify You as I fulfill Your creative purposes invested in me."

Gifts of the Holy Spirit

The Son's Gifts

He ascended on high . . . and gave gifts to men.   Ephesians 4:8

These words, quoted from Psalm 68:18, are employed by the Apostle Paul to call our attention to a special gift-giving ministry of our Lord Jesus Christ Himself. As God's Son, Jesus gave His life for us. While it was the Father's action to "give" or "send" His Son into the world, it was our Lord Jesus' own decision and action to "lay down His life" for us (John 10:15). However, His gift-giving ways proceed beyond His work as *Savior of the World* and also find expression in His work as *Lord of the Church*.

It is as the Church's Builder (Matt. 16:18) that Christ gives additional "gifts to men." These gifts are in the form of people: leaders He anoints and appoints to serve the offices of "apostles, prophets, evangelists, pastors and teachers" (Eph. 4:11). They have been given for the equipping and the edifying of each Christian and each local congregation (Eph. 4:12–16).

This Christmas, think of ways you might indicate your thanks to our Savior for the gift of Christian leaders He has given you.

Gifts of the Holy Spirit

The Spirit's Gifts

There are diversities of gifts, but the same Spirit.

1 Corinthians 12:4

Many scholars today have studied the various listings of spiritual gifts. But their conclusions as to an exact number have varied, not because the Bible is unclear but because it is hard for us to be clear on how gifts "mix." A mix of gifts is what is found in an individual's life when he or she displays, by God's grace, a combination of abilities—in different ways, to different degrees, and at different times.

It is obvious why this "differing" happens. It reflects the unique work of our Creator in fashioning each one of us. It may also reveal the difference in the growth of the individual's learning to apply or exercise his or her gifts.

One category of gifts, however, is much easier to recognize, and they are equally easy to respond to when we learn of them and open ourselves to receive their being manifest through us. They are *the nine gifts of the Holy Spirit* (1 Cor. 12:8–10); a distinct domain of His administration and distribution (1 Cor. 12:11).

Wouldn't it be a joy to become an instrument under the Holy Spirit's power, to be a "delivery agent" for one of His gifts to someone in need this Christmas!

Gifts of the Holy Spirit

The Spirit's Gifts

But earnestly desire the best gifts.   *1 Corinthians 12:31*

Since all nine of the gifts of the Holy Spirit are obviously good, who is to judge which are better or best? It is a proper question, since this verse urges us to become earnestly desirous of "the best," literally to, in a proper sense, "be jealous for the best gift to manifest." How can we make that choice? The answer is that we can't; we don't have to, because the Holy Spirit is fully ready to make that selection.

The Holy Spirit decides *which* gift He wants to be given (or transmitted to someone). He also decides *where* or *for whom* the gift is intended. But He makes these gifts to people through the use of interim "delivery agents"; that is, people who are willing to let Him give His gift *through* them to the intended recipient.

To "earnestly desire the best gifts" can never be understood as long as I view myself as a "recipient and keeper" of a gift of the Holy Spirit. But when I begin to see that He is wanting to use me as an assigned agent, to deliver one of His gifts to someone needing a word, a healing, or a miracle, I can learn to live in a prayerful availability for His use.

Gifts of the Holy Spirit

The Spirit's Gifts

What I do have I give you: In the name of Jesus.   Acts 3:6

*W*e begin to realize the grace of becoming an instrument of God's power when we cease viewing the Spirit's nine gifts as "a collection." These gifts are not cumulative—not *these* nine. Other gifts of God, which define our calling or ministries He gives, these *are* permanent (Rom. 11:29). But the catalog of the Holy Spirit's nine "manifestations" are special graces He is ceaselessly distributing to places and persons where they are needed.

Once a gift is "given" (i.e., once the Holy Spirit finds a person through whom He can distribute a gift), that gift is destined for delivery. In other words, He gives us His gifts to be given away! So remember two things: (1) His gifts are to be given to the person or group He assigns; (2) His gifts are only "giveable" through people who make themselves available—consciously, humbly willing to do so.

Now, in that light, read Acts 3:1–10, and see an example of what happens when "available agents" receive and deliver a gift of the Holy Spirit.

Gifts of Song

You shall have a song as in the night when a holy festival is kept.
Isaiah 30:29

Christmas is a holy festival—the feast of the incarnation of the Son of God, commemorating that "the Word became flesh and dwelt among us" (John 1:14). No event in history has birthed more music than the Feast of Christmas. From "Away in a Manger" to "The Messiah"—from the simplest, most child-like to the most majestically symphonic—the world's "night" has been filled with the festival music of Christmastide.

As we sing the carols of the season, it is a new opportunity to transcend the obvious. The "obvious" lies in our simply singing in observation or celebration of the season. But not so obvious is to see and respond to the fact that the Holy Spirit is present to secure a song in our souls. He is ever ready to implant within us those resources which will make us sufficient for every good work, for every season or circumstance.

The songs of the season pass, but the song which the Spirit seals to you will remain—even when the festival is over.

Gifts of the Holy Spirit

Gifts of Song

You shall surround me with songs of deliverance.   Psalm 32:7

"Deliverance" is one of the giant words of the Scriptures. It is a broadly inclusive term which describes: (1) forgiveness of sin; (2) redemption from eternal death; (3) recovery of physical health; (4) release from spiritual bondage; and (5) rescue from difficult situations. As our Savior, Jesus has become our Deliverer, for the essence of the meaning of salvation is deliverance.

So when we read of "songs of deliverance," we well may tune our souls to the promise and potential of such power being put on human lips. David sang and Saul was relieved of demonic oppression; Jehoshaphat's choir sang and their enemies were conquered; Paul and Silas sang and an earthquake shook their bonds free and their captor into God's kingdom. Songs of deliverance are real instruments of divine grace.

As the carols of Christmas fill the air, let each one be more than a ritual. Lift these testimonies of the King who has come, and let the Holy Spirit fill your praise until they become songs of deliverance—for the King is here!

Christmas Kings

Herod the king . . . was troubled.   Matthew 2:3

We should not be surprised at the dynamic tension Christmas creates. On the one hand, our world fills its stores in commercial pursuit, while on the other it argues our right to put nativity scenes in public squares. It is the way of the world spirit to want the profit and resist the prophecies.

When Herod met the regal wise men who seemed to promise commerce from the East, he was ready to assist their journey. It was good business to cooperate with wealthy men travelling through his territory. But when he discovered their journey had been prompted by prophecies of another king, Herod was troubled.

Don't be distracted by the misconceptions or distortions of the world spirit at Christmastime. And may we never become embittered by that spirit's protests—its being "troubled" by our pursuit of the King and by our desire to worship Him.

Simply stay on course. The pathway to Bethlehem may be doubted by the world, but it is still the pathway to hope and salvation for all who believe.

Gifts of the Holy Spirit

Christmas Kings

When they had come into the house, they . . . fell down and worshiped Him.
                                                          Matthew 2:11

The term "kings" is not actually used concerning the magi—the wise men—who were actually counselors from the court of ancient kings. But their royal role, and the possibility that they were formal representatives of a distant throne, gives allowance for our tradition of calling them kings.

Our frequent note of their gifts might overlook the most notable fact about them. Before mentioning their gifts, the Bible says that when they saw Jesus, they "fell down and worshiped Him." It is after that that they "opened their treasures."

When the precise wording is read and the sequence studied—falling down, worshiping, giving—don't you wonder what really happened? This was no casual issue—nor was it merely a pageant-like, formal moment. These men were overwhelmed, doubtless encountering a presence they did not expect.

May that same presence overwhelm us this Christmastime.

Gifts of the Holy Spirit

Christmas Kings

Of His kingdom there will be no end. *Luke 1:33*

From the time of Jesus' conception a stream of promise begins to flow: a new government is coming to the souls of men! The issue was not political, but spiritual. The King Himself verifies this: "My kingdom is not of this world" (John 18:36).

But He is King, a king like no other. Look at the descriptions of His kingly role in God's Word:

• "The King eternal" (1 Tim. 1:17)—as such, the endlessness, the unchanging durability of His rule is declared.

• "A king will reign in righteousness" (Is. 32:1)—as such, His completely just, even-handed, considerate and life-releasing method is forecast.

• "King of peace" (Heb. 7:2)—as typified in Melchizedek and fulfilled through His rising to His first throne, the cross, where He secured our peace (Eph. 2:14–18).

• "King of the saints" and "King of kings" (Rev. 15:3; 19:16)—forever praised as our saving King, and all history's ultimate Ruler!

Gifts of the Holy Spirit

Back to Bethlehem

But you, Bethlehem . . . out of you shall come a Ruler.

Matthew 2:6

ven its pronunciation is musical—"Bethlehem." The name itself sets the imagination aflame again, as we all experience the symphony of thoughts about this tiny, yet mightily historic site. Bethlehem was destined for significance by the Almighty God Himself. He whispered His intent to His prophets, and in our text we hear Micah quoted more than seven hundred years after he predicted Bethlehem would be the Messiah's birthplace.

It is a good thing to go there—at least in our imagination; and especially at Christmastime. The fact that God would interest Himself in so tiny a village, and ordain its place and high purpose in His plan of redemption, tells us something about God and His ways.

He delights to take the ordinary and do the extraordinary there. He loves to take people like us and do wonderful things *for* them, *to* them, and *through* them. It is His mind and His pleasure to do great things at simple places, with plain people! Just as we sing, so let us act: "Come to Bethlehem and see!"

Gifts of the Holy Spirit

Back to Bethlehem

Joseph [with Mary] went to the city of David, which is called Bethlehem.

Luke 2:4

In a poignant, soul-stirring way, it is interesting to watch the management of our sovereign God as He makes Bethlehem a crossroads of human history. He moves the Emperor of Rome to pass an edict which will result in Joseph's return to his family's hometown—and, thereby, Jesus will be born there. He moves the stars and planets to a unique convergence which will prompt a group of eastern courtiers to study this phenomenon in conjunction with ancient Scriptures and come to worship at Bethlehem. He arranges for a crowded inn, so that His Son, forced to a birth arrival in a stable, will never be accused of having been advantaged through "high" birth.

None of these things happened by accident. They were arranged, strategized and executed by the God of the universe. And as we come back to Bethlehem this Christmas, it is our wisdom to think on these things. In doing so, remember that He's equally interested in assuring the success of the affairs of your life.

Back to Bethlehem

When they saw the star, they rejoiced. Matthew 2:10

Have you noticed how people designate the star that shone with splendor at Christmas? It is called "the star of Bethlehem"—not "the Jesus star," "the Christmas star," "the Judean star," or some other name. This light, which beamed earthward from astronomical distances beyond our planet, is named for a dusty little village without distinction, except . . . except that *Jesus was born there!*

Would you let that become a Christmas gift-thought to you—a thought that may keep on giving if you allow it to. It is another pointer to the ways that God has of dignifying, enabling, and advancing His grace upon each of us in whom Jesus has been born!

Just as you would find Bethlehem a profitable business center today, because Christ was born there, so God is willing to ordain fruitfulness for each of us in whom Jesus lives. The Bethlehem starfire has ignited His glory over you, loved one: "Arise, shine; for . . . the glory of the Lord is risen upon you" (Is. 60:1)!

Gifts of the Holy Spirit

Christmas Glory

The gift of God is eternal life.   *Romans 6:23*

Understandable excitement filled the house this Christmas Eve. All the children and the grandchildren were there, gathered from points far and near. A festive yet holy atmosphere filled the room as lights were dimmed and only multi-colored Christmas tree lights now twinkled. Presents would soon be unwrapped, but first, at the gentle beckoning of Grandpa's hand, the room quieted to the very youngest grandchild.

Smiling, Grandpa began, as all harmonized with him in song: ". . . so loved He the world that He gave us His Son." Then all worshipfully bowed as Grandpa prayed:

"Precious Father, before we open our gifts tonight, first we thank You for the greatest gift, Jesus, Your Son, our Savior. In the light of this tree, we are reminded of the tree, the cross, where Your gift of eternal life was presented to us. So, from the foot of this tree, we bow at the foot of the one from which the Light of the world sheds Your glory to all of us. Please be praised, O Lord, as our giving in love here remembers Your Gift of Love there. Amen."

Christmas Glory

Born to you this day . . . a Savior.   *Luke 2:11*

Our finest authors and composers have written their most magnificently when taking the theme of Christmas. But though ten thousand marvelous stories and songs are at our disposal, all across the face of the planet on this day millions of hands turn to the pages of Luke's timeless record of Jesus' birth. Chapter 2, verses 1–20, not only root the coming of Christ in history (in the days of Caesar Augustus), but they target Christ's birth on our present moment: "to you this day."

The angelic message, delivered to men at their work place, could not be more eloquent in its simplicity: "To you . . . today . . . a Savior." Then His title is given (Christ the Lord) and the pathway to His side is related (to Bethlehem).

So it is that we have come to know Him as: Christ our Lord and as Jesus, the Son of God. And we have come to His side, not only to kneel in humility at a manger, but to worship with gratitude here, praising at the side of Him, who later from His side, paid the blood-price to win His role as Savior and to purchase our gift of eternal salvation.

Gifts of the Holy Spirit

Post-Christmas Travel

They departed for their own country another way. Matthew 2:12

oday airline terminals pulsate to the returning foot-steps of Christmastime visitors en route to their homes. Most everyone is using the second half of a round-trip ticket. Yet most of us know that to change that routing usually will involve paying extra fare.

The wise men planned a round-trip, but they changed their route. The Bible does not tell us which way they went, but it does tell us why they changed their plan. "Being divinely warned," it reads—lead by the Holy Spirit to take a path which averted becoming captured by Herod who had deceived them.

As we "leave" Christmas this year, it may be wise to invite the Holy Spirit to help us leave "another way." Allowing Him to soften our hearts, alter our priorities, clarify our understanding, cleanse our hearts—all point us "another way" than the way we came to Christmas. And on His path we will avoid the enemy's snares. It is the wise man's way.

Gifts of the Holy Spirit

New Year's Countdown

Love . . . hopes all things.   *1 Corinthians 13:4–8*

Today, begin a "countdown" to the beginning of the New Year. Let each point—each day—become a milestone as you "depart another way," leaving the past behind and welcoming the Holy Spirit's ministry to bring a glorious newness to your soul. These days, let us look at the themes of love, power, transformation, the Word, and faith: milestone markers.

Open this day and these days with a full-hearted, special welcome to the Holy Spirit to *flush,* to *fill* and to *flow* through your heart with love. He can and will send a surge of love, according to God's Word (Rom. 5:5). It will come in gushing, rushing rivers (John 7:37–39) and remove every obstruction to our being perfected in a love for Christ, a love for God's Word, a love for the lost, a love for the unlovely, and a love for those who have wounded us. He changes our attitude and outlook—hope for tomorrow becomes more than a wish. Love begets a hope that is confident.

Gifts of the Holy Spirit

New Year's Countdown

Paul, filled with the Holy Spirit . . .   *Acts 13:9*

Power: The power of *the Holy Spirit. Filled* with the power of the Holy Spirit. These are three completely different issues. Power, ability or authority, is wielded daily in every arena of life. The Holy Spirit's power is also, for He's at work everywhere. But the Spirit's power operates and manifests in vastly different ways than mere "power" as exercised in our society.

"Filled" is the word which describes the one kind of person the Holy Spirit is most able to lead, to use, and to make effective in this needy world. We need more than "power," we need to be filled with the Holy Spirit's power.

Paul's encounter with evil powers in Cyprus (Acts 13) turned to a victory for God's kingdom, and the pivotal reason was Paul's present fullness. He was "living full" of the Holy Spirit.

Approaching the New Year, mark well the difference between having *had* an experience in the Holy Spirit and *living* in the fullness of His power.

New Year's Countdown

But we all . . . are being transformed.   2 Corinthians 3:18

The Bible gives a context to the liberated life: "Where the Spirit of the Lord is, there is liberty!" But it quickly describes exactly how the Holy Spirit works to create and sustain the freedom of His Kingdom. Study this amplification of our text.

"But we all (everyone of us deciding for ourselves), with unveiled face (not hiding behind pretense or cowering from God's dealings with us), beholding as in a mirror (which is the Word of God) the glory of the Lord (which is the Son of God), are being transformed (that is, progressing from stage to stage as a creature undergoes metamorphosis—a caterpillar to a cocoon to a butterfly) into the same image (of Jesus, our Master, Model, and Savior) from glory to glory (or from one stage of His grace and character to ever-expanding dimensions of the same) just as by the Spirit of the Lord (for it is only by His presence, power, and perfecting work that such a change can happen!)."

Anyone willing to be freed and changed that way is destined to a great new year!

New Year's Countdown

Receive with meekness the implanted word.   James 1:21

*G*od's Word is the source of *wisdom* for living, the standard of holiness for *character*, and the strength of the human spirit as *truth*. This Book, breathed by the Holy Spirit, is the foundation for our building, the fortress for our defense, and the food for our sustenance. Too much cannot be said about God's Word.

But too little can be done.

Only as I feed daily, and only as I receive in humility what the Word says about me, does this divine masterpiece take effect. The Pharisees of Jesus' time were experts in knowing the Word but failures in receiving it. So, on the brink of a New Year, lay plans for reading through the Word. But also plan to let it read through you too. Its saving power, which saves us from confusion, error, and failure just as surely as its truth saves our eternal souls, depends on such reception.

New Year's Countdown

Look up . . . redemption draws near. Luke 21:28

Just as certainly as we are people of the Book, we are also consummately a people of the Hope. One sure sign of a Holy Spirit-filled person is that he or she not only believes Jesus is coming, they live in hope, with expectation of His coming.

And such faith does not only see His second coming as the whole of their hope. Of course, Jesus' return is our highest hope, but faith-filled people believe that the King is ready to come today, to enter life's circumstance with a visitation of His kingdom grace, love, and power!

Zechariah, one of the greatest prophets of the Messiah's return, said, "Return to the stronghold, you prisoners of hope" (Zech. 9:12). He spoke literally of a people who were imprisoned, that is, "shut up unto" hope. What a concept: to be inescapably bound to the confidence that our Redeemer is coming today to meet us with His grace fully sufficient, and that He is coming soon to take us to eternal glory! Happy New Year!

Gifts of the Holy Spirit